HULTON'S PICTURE HISTORIES

GENERAL EDITOR: EDWARD HULTON

English Pottery

A

A Collection of underglaze coloured earthenware, made by Pratt, Wedgwood and other Staffordshire and Yorkshire potteries *c.* 1775-1815.

A Picture History of

English Pottery

Griselda Lewis

Hulton Press: London

FIRST PUBLISHED 1956

Printed in Great Britain by The Chiswick Press, N.11

Contents

Introduction

English pottery is an endearing subject. It seems to cover the whole range of human emotions and human tastes. It varies from a simple crudity and rustic simplicity to extreme sophistication. Apart from the cultivated perfection of Wedgwood's agate and Jasper wares, there is also an underlying vein of humour which irresistibly keeps bubbling to the surface. One has only to think of the medieval jugs decorated with comic human faces, or of the Toft slipware charger of Royalty *in extremis* in the Boscobel Oak or of the Lambeth 'blue dash' Delft charger picturing Adam and Eve exchanging the fruit of the tree of knowledge which looks for all the world like a glorified humbug! This humorous quality is, of course, particularly obvious in the figures and chimney piece ornaments; from the delightfully amusing salt glazed pew groups to Astbury's little bandsmen and the figures of Whieldon, Pratt, Walton, Salt and Sherratt and on to the Sampson Smith 'cottage pots'. Humour is also not lacking in much of the work of our studio potters today. Mr. Vergette's striped cats are certainly in this tradition.

This native humour is only one aspect of English pottery, but it seems in some ways to typify the people of the potteries and the atmosphere of the five towns. On our visits to many potteries, we have been struck by the warm-heartedness of the potters. And much of their kindliness seems to have found its way into their pots, which have been thrown, cast or decorated with a loving indulgence.

The choice of subjects illustrated in this book has been governed by a wish to show pieces of pottery that have not been illustrated before. This wish has inevitably been tempered by the fact that certain widely known pieces are an integral part of English pottery history. Much less space has been given to the salt glazed Whieldon and Ralph Wood figures than they really deserve. Inevitably, too, such a selection only touches the fringes, for it is a subject of unending variations and delights and new discoveries. For instance the magnificent thirteenth-century green glazed 'rope handled' jug decorated with little knights in armour, illustrated in fig 12, was only discovered a few months ago in a digging on a bombed site in Nottingham, and we are proud to say it makes its first appearance to a wider public in this book.

English pottery is a subject which would make most historians despair, for though practically every pottery firm has its roots in the past, and every piece of English pottery has some kind of historical connotation, the documentary evidence is pitifully small. The collector and the student have to trust to their own eyes. It is only by constant observation and handling that one begins to get the feel of good pottery—and good pottery can have been made at any time, including today.

The fairly large showing given here to modern studio potters, we think is justified by the fact that much of the modern work will bear comparison with work of the past, and collectors might well realize that one day it is possible that these pieces will be collected quite as eagerly as are the pieces by Astbury, Wood and Whieldon today.

Finally the contribution of the great modern pottery factories—a contribution largely of mass produced traditional forms and decorations, though lacking something of the quality of the eighteenth-century ware, can be more than justified by the gigantic markets served, and the value for money that modern English pottery gives.

I
Early Bronze Age Beaker *c.* 1900-1400 B.C. from Goodmanham, East Riding, Yorkshire. Height 6¾″

I. Early Pottery in Britain

FROM THE BRONZE AGE TO THE REIGN OF QUEEN ELIZABETH I

The earliest English pottery belongs to the New Stone Age (*c.* 2500-1900 B.C.). Though it has come down to us as mere fragments, archaeologists have been able to build up conjectural restorations of various shapes of cooking vessels with rounded bases, suitable for standing in a hollow on the ground. It is not until the Early Bronze Age that we know for certain what the early British pots were really like.

The pottery that survives from the Bronze Age (*c.* 1900-450 B.C.) is often in a well-preserved state, for it was buried deliberately with the ashes of the dead. The Bronze Age cinerary urns, made to hold these cremated remains probably did not differ much from the household cooking and storage pots of the time. The beakers and urns of this period, though shaped by hand were well formed and decorated with incised patterns of herringbone or cross-hatched bands, made with a pointed stick, or sometimes with lines made by the impressing of a cord or thong, or patterns made with a fingernail.

The potter's wheel was introduced into this country during the last phase of the Early Iron Age (somewhere about 75 B.C.) and, dating from this period, are well thrown though rather clumsy shapes, ornamented with wheel-turned decorations.

When the Romans first came to Britain, they imported a quantity of red-gloss pottery from Gaul, Italy and the Rhineland; but soon Roman potters (no doubt aided by the native English) were at work in England and the red-gloss ware was produced at any rate at Colchester in Essex, though of a much poorer quality than that made in Italy.

At about the beginning of the second century A.D. a

distinctive type of pottery was made at Castor, near Peterborough in Northamptonshire. Some of this was of a light-bodied earthenware of varying hardness, and a dark purplish red colour; it was often decorated with slip of the same colour, trailed on to the surface, like cake icing, in abstract scroll patterns or animal forms. The most attractive ware made at Castor had a smooth black body and was decorated with white slip. It was surprisingly thin and delicately potted. Castor ware was made until the late fourth or early fifth century A.D. At the same time pottery of a similar type was made in other places, notably in the New Forest; but useful ware of all kinds including storage jars, cooking pots, mortars for grinding corn and feeding bottles must have been produced in considerable quantities wherever potteries existed.

After the retreat of the Romans from these islands, a period of lawlessness and disorder prevailed. The British seem to have spent all their energies on keeping alive and defending their homes and families from various foreign invaders. What pottery survives from this time is of a strictly utilitarian nature and coarsely made. The influence of the Roman potters appears to be forgotten.

The domestic pottery of medieval England was much less refined than that produced at the time of the Roman occupation. The most usual pottery vessels were jugs and pitchers, for at this time the common people ate from wooden platters and drank from vessels made of horn or wood, whereas the nobility and the rich merchants used metal plates, jugs and cups. Pottery was mostly confined to the kitchen or to the peasants' hut. Even so, the pieces that have been preserved for us to this day can hardly be dismissed as uninteresting. They may be crude, but they are remarkable for their bold shapes and the diversity of their decoration. The jugs and pitchers of the thirteenth century tended to be rather tall and attenuated, whereas those of the fourteenth century became broader in the base and less high. Some of the ware was left unglazed and undecorated, but much was patterned with a different coloured slip, or with incised lines, or decorated with reliefs stamped in different coloured clays, which were made with a wooden stamp cut in intaglio.

The only known glaze at that time had a lead basis, and developed a yellowish colour in the firing. Sometimes this glaze was stained with copper, giving it a variety of greens, and some of the later wares were coated with slip stained with manganese, which produced a rich dark brown when glazed with lead. The glaze was sprinkled, or dusted on the surface with a rag. Sometimes it was confined to only part of a vessel. Many jugs have just a 'bib' of glaze under the spout. Owing to the primitive methods of firing pottery in medieval times, impurities were always present in the kilns, and this accounts for the generally dark appearance of the ware.

In addition to domestic ware, tiles were made for the decoration of the walls and pavements of churches and abbeys. The designs on these tiles were either incised or impressed, modelled in low relief or inlaid, or occasionally decorated with slip. They were often glazed.

Much of the ware of Tudor times, though rather coarse, is glazed with a green stained lead glaze. The objects that have been found range from candlesticks to chamber pots.

During the first half of the sixteenth century—that is up to 1540, when Henry VIII ordered the dissolution of the monasteries, a particularly good ware was made. This has been given the name 'Cistercian' ware, because pieces have been found in the ruins of the Cistercian abbeys in Yorkshire, though wasters of a similar pottery have been found in places all over the country as far apart as Ely and Abergavenny; it is also known that it was still being made during the seventeenth century. The ware is quite thin and smooth, has a hard red body, fired almost to stoneware hardness, and is covered with a lead glaze stained to a purplish brown with manganese. Drinking vessels with one or more handles known as tygs, are typical of this ware.

British Museum

An illustration from the Luttrell Psalter *c* 1340 AD

2   *Victoria & Albert Museum*

3   *Victoria & Albert Museum*

4   *Victoria & Albert Museum*

5   *Guildhall Museum*

2. Middle Bronze Age Urn with overhanging rim *c.* 1400-1000 B.C. from Kempston, Bedfordshire.   Height 8″

3. Early Iron Age (third period) Pedestal Urn *c.* 75 B.C. This has been thrown on a wheel. From the cremation cemetery, Aylesford, Kent.   Height 9¾″

4. Early Iron Age (third period) Butt Beaker *c.* 75 B.C. with wheel turned and rouletted decoration. From Sutton Courtney, Berkshire.   Height 6¾″

5. Castor ware Cup with barbotine decoration, showing a dog chasing a stag. Second or third century A.D. Found in Jewry Street, Aldgate.   Height 2½″

6. Castor ware Vase or Beaker, black with white slip decoration. Third century A.D. Found in Broad Street, London.   Height 5⅝″

6   *Guildhall Museum*

7

9

7. These Lead Glazed Red Tiles, inlaid with white clay are from Chertsey Abbey. The architecture of the canopies above the Queen, Bishop and King in the three long panels is in the style of the late thirteenth century, which puts their date about 1275.   Height 31″

8. The Circular Tile from Chertsey Abbey seems to be of a slightly earlier date than the oblong panels above. It shows King Richard in single combat with the Sultan Saladin at Babylon.
          16″ square

9. This Circular Tile from Chertsey Abbey shows the King of Ireland demanding children as tribute from King Mark.   Dia. 9½″

8

Guildhall Museum

10. Baluster Jug, with traces of a yellowish glaze. *c.* 1275. Found in Blossoms Inn Yard, Lawrence Lane, London. Height 18″

Fitzwilliam Museum

Nottingham Museum

12. This handsome Jug has recently been found in Nottingham, in a medieval midden, on the site of the Old Moot Hall, Friar Lane. The building on this site received a direct hit by enemy aircraft during the 1939-45 war.

Though unfortunately the jug was broken, there was quite enough left to be able to restore it to its exact former shape. From the site where it was found and from the type of shields carried by the knights in armour which encircle the neck, it can be dated as any time between 1275-1325. The body of the jug is decorated in low relief with a design of stags attacked by hounds. The 'rope' handle is extremely interesting. The jug is made of a buff coloured clay, glazed with a very good dark apple green lead glaze. Height 14″

11. Jug decorated with incised and rouletted patterns, and glazed with a yellowish green glaze. Thirteenth or fourteenth century. Found at Scarborough. Height 14⅝″

13   *Nottingham Museum*

Buff earthenware Pitcher with brownish yellow lead glaze merging to green below. Purple black stripes. Found on a kiln site in Nottingham. *c* 1300-1400.   Height 20″

14   *Guildhall Museum*

Red earthenware Jug with decoration trailed on in white slip under a yellow lead glaze. Found at Austin Friars London *c*. 1300.   Height 14¾″

15   *Guildhall Museum*

Buff Jug with green and brown decoration under a yellow lead glaze. Found in Bishopsgate Street, London. *c*. 1300-1400.   Height 11″

16   *Fitzwilliam Museum*

Dark Buff Jug with a mottled green glaze. Found in London. Fourteenth century.   Height 11¼″

17   *Fitzwilliam Museum*

Red Pitcher with white slip applied decoration, glazed with a lead glaze. Fourteenth century.   Height 8¾″

18   *Fitzwilliam Museum*

Red earthenware Jug with speckled green glaze over a 'bib' of white slip. Found at Clerkenwell, London. Fourteenth century.

        Height 8¾″

19. Red-brown earthenware Watering Pot, partly glazed with a yellow lead glaze. Sixteenth century.   Height 10½″

20. Puzzle Jug of light red earthenware with a coating of white slip covered with a mottled dark green glaze. The date 1571 is applied in strips of clay.   Height 11¼″

21. Watering Pot of dark red-brown earthenware with a design in white slip. Late fifteenth century. It was filled by submersion in water which was then retained by holding the thumb over the hole in the top. When the thumb was removed the water poured out through the holes in the base.   Height 11¼″

22. Candle Bracket of pale buff coloured earthenware with a yellow lead glaze. Late sixteenth century.　　Height 17½″

23. Two-handled Tyg, or drinking cup made of hard red earthenware with a black glaze. Early seventeenth century.
　　　　　　　　　　　Height 5¾″
　This is very much the same as the 'Cistercian' ware, so called from its appearance in the ruins of the Cistercian Abbeys. This was made from the beginning of the sixteenth century.

24. Tall Mug. This is covered with a smooth olive green glaze. It was found on the site of Crosby Hall, Bishopsgate, London. Sixteenth or seventeenth century.　　　　　　　　　Height 5″

25
Blue Dash Charger, with a portrait of George II. Made in Bristol *c.* 1740.

Dia. 13¼″

II. Delft Ware

TIN ENAMELLED EARTHENWARE C. 1550-1800

Tin enamelled earthenware, or delft ware as it is often called, is an earthenware covered with an opaque whitish glaze made from oxide of tin. It was made in Syria, Asia Minor and Egypt as early as the sixth century A.D. It was first made in Europe by the Moors in Spain, then by the Italians. This technique finally arrived in England, by way of the Netherlands, in the mid-sixteenth century. The main centres of production in this country were London, Bristol and Liverpool.

Though the Dutch had learned their tin glazing technique from the Italians, their actual manner of decoration was more frequently copied from the oriental porcelain then being imported by the Dutch East India Company than from the decorations on Italian maiolica.

The English manufacturers of delft ware never perhaps reached the high degree of artistic perfection that the Dutch had achieved, but they added something to the foreign designs which prevented them from being mere slavish copies.

The earliest English delft pieces were jugs, mottled with various colours, and similar in shape to the German stoneware that was imported into this country at that time. These early jugs were sometimes mounted in silver, which was hall-marked, and so the pieces are dated, some as early as 1550. One such jug, hall-marked 1581-82, came from the church at West Malling in Kent and two others have been found in that neighbourhood. No traces of a kiln, however, have been found, and in all probability these 'Malling' jugs (as they have come to be called) were made in London.

In 1571, two Flemish potters called Jacob Janson and Jasper Andries sent a petition to Queen Elizabeth, asking permission to settle by the banks of the Thames. They are said to have produced delft ware at a pottery near Aldgate.

A delft ware pottery was started in Southwark about 1625 and from there some craftsmen travelled to the west country and settled just outside Bristol, where the Brislington pottery was founded about 1650. Other potteries making tin glazed earthenware soon grew up in the neighbourhood.

Chinese porcelain was being imported into England by the mid-seventeenth century, but it was extremely expensive and only within the reach of the rich. The delft ware of the English potters of this period was an attempt to provide the middle classes who could not afford Chinese porcelain, with the best imitation that they were able to make, for although delft ware was often thick and always completely opaque, it certainly bore a superficial resemblance to Chinese porcelain.

A tremendous variety of articles were manufactured. Wine jars, puzzle jugs, fuddling cups, hand and boot warmers, plates, dishes, mugs, candlesticks, posset pots; bleeding bowls, drug jars and pill slabs for the apothecary, tiles and even ornaments. The choice of decoration was very varied and often the only colour used was blue, derived from cobalt. Sometimes this would be combined with a decoration in white on a pale bluish or greyish ground—a particularly attractive technique known as 'white on white' or 'bianco sopra bianco', as it was of Italian origin. This particular type of decoration was used from about the middle of the eighteenth century at Lambeth and Bristol. The later delft designs were often painted with several colours. Green, brick-red, brown, yellow and purple were used to produce rich and varied effects.

The first Lambeth delft ware pottery is thought to date from about 1665. It became the largest centre for the production of this ware and continued working until the end of the eighteenth century. Typical Lambeth productions were wine bottles often with the name and sometimes the date of the contents, pill slabs and drug jars and large shallow bowls or chargers decorated with dashes of blue round the rim and with formalized fruit or flower designs, scenes of the Fall, and portraits of sovereigns. Dishes were also made with the arms of the various Liveried Companies.

At Bristol, chargers and plates were made on the lines of the Lambeth ware. It is extremely difficult to say exactly which pottery produced each piece, sometimes the comparison of a piece with fragments found on the site will help in the identification.

The first dated piece of Liverpool delft is a large plaque inscribed 'A West Prospect of Great Crosby 1716', but the first mention of pottery at Liverpool occurs in a list of town dues payable at the port in 1674, which contains the following item: 'For every cartload of mugs (shipped) into foreign ports 6d.; for every cartload of mugs along the coast 4d.; for every crate of cupps or pipes along the coast 1d.'

In the *Transactions of the Historical Society of Lancashire and Cheshire*, 3 May 1855, there is an interesting account by Dr. Joseph Mayer of a potter, Zachariah Barnes, making delft at Liverpool in the latter half of the eighteenth century, when its use had been superseded in most of the country by salt-glazed stoneware and later by cream coloured earthenware. Dr. Mayer wrote: 'Amongst other articles were very large round dishes, chiefly sent into Wales, where the simple habits of their forefathers remained unchanged long after their alteration in England; and the master of the house and his guests dipped their spoons into the mess and helped themselves from the dish placed in the middle of the table. Quantities of this ware were sent to the great border fairs, held at Chester, whither the inhabitants of the more remote and inaccessible parts of the mountain districts of Wales assembled, to buy their stores for the year. This continued until a very recent time. . . .'

Delft ware was made for a short time at Wincanton in Somerset from 1736 and also in the eighteenth century, in Glasgow and Ireland.

Picture Post Library

An illustration from Commenius Orbis Sensualium pictus (English Edition 1659)

26   *Guildhall Museum*

Jug of the 'Malling' type, covered with a rich blue glaze. Possibly made in London in the second half of the sixteenth century.   Height 6″

27   *Fitzwilliam Museum*

Round Dish with a decoration in the Italian style. The man on the galloping horse is probably intended to be Charles II, when Prince of Wales. Made in Lambeth about 1645.   Dia. 12¾″

28   *Fitzwilliam Museum*

Round Dish, painted in blue and brownish orange. The back of the dish is glazed with a transparent lead glaze. Made in Lambeth about 1650. Dia. 15⅝″

29   *Fitzwilliam Museum*

Mug, painted in blue on a white ground. Round the neck are the names IOHN POTTEN & SUSANNA 1633. Made in Lambeth.   Height 5⅜″

30. Puzzle Jug, painted in blue on a white ground. Inscribed c
W E
1653. It was the custom at that time to put the initial of the surname first, followed by the christian name initials of the couple to whom the vessel was inscribed. Made in Lambeth.   Height 6⅝″

31. Drug Pot, decorated in purple and blue on a white ground. Probably made in Lambeth in the seventeenth century.   Height 4½″

32 Sauce Boat in the form of a bath holding a recumbent figure of Pomona. Painted in blue, orange and manganese purple. The design has been copied from a French original by Bernard Palissy. Made about 1650 at Lambeth.
Length 8″

30   *Fitzwilliam Museum*

31   *Guildhall Museum*   32   *Fitzwilliam Museum*

33 *Nottingham Museum*

Large dish moulded in relief. The design is taken from a dish made by Bernard Palissy, who copied the subject from a painting by Titian, called La Fecondité. Painted in blue, copper green, yellow and manganese purple. Made at Lambeth about 1665. Length 18½″

34 *Fitzwilliam Museum*

Vessel in the form of a man with a pipe, painted in blue, orange and turquoise. Under the base there is the inscription M 1675. Made at Lambeth. Height 9⅛″

35 *Fitzwilliam Museum*

Wine Jug, painted in blue, orange and yellow. Made at Lambeth 1660. Height 7″

36   *Victoria & Albert Museum*

Charger with portrait of James II in the centre. Light blue-green enamel ground. There are other chargers almost identical to this one (even to the position of the eyes) marked Charles II. They were made in London between 1660 and the end of the century.
Dia. 13¼″

37   *Fitzwilliam Museum*

Charger with blue dash border and decoration in blue, olive green, yellow and black. The back of the dish is covered with a transparent greenish glaze. Early eighteenth century. Perhaps made at Lambeth.
Dia. 13½″

38   *Fitzwilliam Museum*

Plate. Painted in blue on a white ground. Made at Lambeth about 1725.
Dia. 8¾″

39   *Mrs John Lewis*

Plate with blue decoration on a white ground. It is amusing to see a pottery kiln drawn in the Chinese style. Made probably at Lambeth in the eighteenth century.
Dia. 8¾″

40   Punch Bowl, painted in blue on a white ground. Probably made in Bristol about 1715.   Dia. 10¼″   *Fitzwilliam Museum*

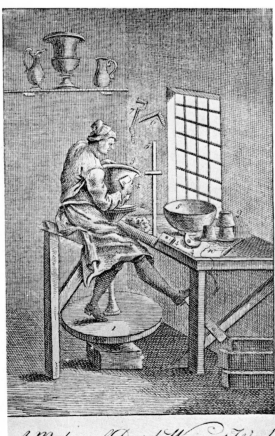

A Maker of Dutch-Ware at Work

41   *Fitzwilliam Museum*

Posset Pot with lid. Painted in blue on a white ground. On one side there are the initials J.H., on the other the date 1700. The lid does not match the pot. Both probably made at Bristol.

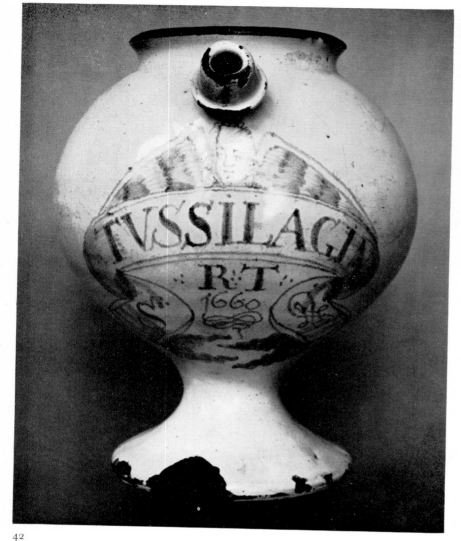

42

43

42. Apothecary's Jar. Made in Lambeth in 1660.
Height 8¼″

43. Plate, covered with a bluish white enamel and painted over in blue and opaque white. Made by Joseph Flower at Redcliffe Back, Bristol; about 1750.
Dia. of plate 8⅞″

44. Teapot with attached lid. (It is filled through a hole in the bottom on the inkwell principle, in the manner of the Cadogan teapots.) Probably made at Joseph Flower's pottery at Bristol, about 1750.
Height 5⅝″

45. Mug, probably painted by John Bowen at the pottery of Joseph Flower. The inscription reads: 'MARY TURNER AGED 2 YEARS 14 DAYS SEPr 2 1752.
Height 3¾″

44

45

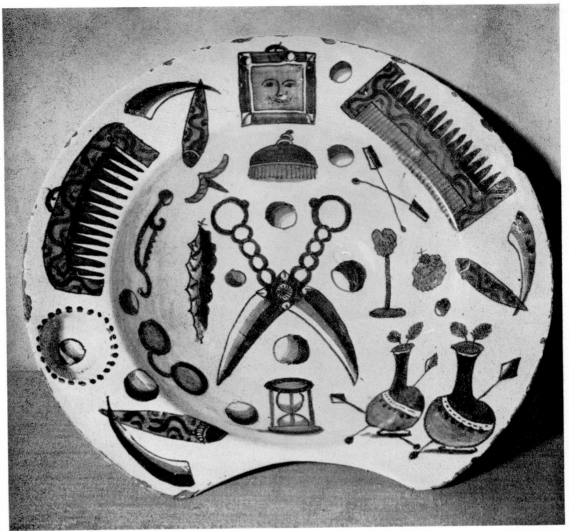

Nottingham Museum

46. Barber's Dish painted in blue on a white ground, with a design incorporating all the tools of a barber's trade. Made at Lambeth *c.* 1690.

Dia. 10⅜″

47. Tile, painted in blue with details in green and red. Made at Bristol some time during the first half of the eighteenth century. 5″ sq.

48. Tile, pale lavender coloured with flowers in opaque white. Made in Bristol by Joseph Flower about 1760. 5″ sq.

Fitzwilliam Museum

Fitzwilliam Museum

49

Punch Bowl. Painted in blue, yellow, brownish red, manganese purple and green. Made in Liverpool about 1760.   Dia. 14″

50   *Fitzwilliam Museum*

Large circular Dish made by Ralph Toft, Staffordshire. *c.* 1670-80.   Dia. 17¼″

III. *Slipware*

LEAD GLAZED AND SLIP DECORATED EARTHENWARE OF THE 17TH AND 18TH CENTURIES

Although slip decoration was used by the Romans and during medieval times, this method was not exploited to the full until the second decade of the seventeenth century and it continued in use throughout the eighteenth. It was still employed by various country potters in the nineteenth century, and today the old methods of this type of decoration have been used with varying degrees of success by many studio potters.

Slipware, as it has come to be called, was made principally in and around London, at Wrotham in Kent and in Staffordshire, as well as many other districts in which pottery was made including Buckinghamshire, Cambridgeshire (Ely), Derbyshire (Tickenhall), Bolsover near Chesterfield, North Devon (Bideford, Fremington and Barnstaple), Gestingthorpe in Essex, Fareham in Hampshire, High Halden in Kent, Nottingham, Somerset

(Donyatt), Pill near Bristol; Sussex (Rye, Chailey and East Grinstead), Dicker near Hellingly, Polesworth in Warwickshire and South Wiltshire in and around Salisbury. In Yorkshire at Halifax, Burton-in-Lonsdale and during the nineteenth century at Bradshaw, also in the same century at Bridgend and Ewenny in Glamorganshire and Castle Hedingham in Essex.

The earliest known marked piece is dated 1612, but dated pieces are rare until the second half of the seventeenth century.

The basic material, the clay fired to different shades of brown or red, or a buff coloured clay, remained crude and coarse in contrast with some of the decoration—notably the marbling and feathering which was often very skilfully done. Also the pieces decorated with trailed slip, though often naïve in the extreme in conception, are remarkably

51   *Fitzwilliam Museum*

Staffordshire slipware circular dish made by Thomas Toft *c.* 1670-80   Dia. 21″
The decoration shows an incorrect version of the Royal Arms of England with supporters,
crowned helmet and mantling, motto and Garter, and the initials C.R. (King Charles II.)
The name of the maker Thomas Toft appears below the motto.

well carried out, the technique of dotting and trailing and trellising the slip being extremely difficult. The designs in sgraffito, that is the design scratched through a layer of slip to show the different coloured body beneath, also show both in pattern and technique, the skill and artistic ability of their makers.

A great diversity of objects were made in slipware, from the large and handsome round dishes of Thomas Toft and his contemporaries, to simple little mugs and tygs. Fuddling cups, puzzle jugs, posset pots and candlesticks of complex design, cradles, salt-kits and teapots; baking dishes with combed and marbled patterns, jugs and money-boxes are all to be found.

The colourings are always similar—trailings of white slip or slip stained dark brown with manganese, or red with iron oxide, or occasionally green with copper, are laid on the brown, red or buff body of the ware over which there is a yellowish lead glaze, so the basic effect is brown and yellow.

52. Large Circular Dish made by George Taylor in Staffordshire. The body is light red earthenware coated with white slip, the decoration is in dark red slip dotted with white. The solid parts are light red. The whole is covered with a yellow lead glaze. The back of the dish is left unglazed. The figure on the right is probably Charles II and his companion is perhaps his wife, Catherine of Braganza. *c.* 1680.   Dia. 17¾″

53. Large Circular Dish from the Wrotham factory. The white slip has been cut away to make the design, exposing the light red clay below. The dish is glazed with a yellowish glaze mottled green in places.

                            Dia. 17⅞″

54. Two-handled Tyg. Made in or near London in the mid-seventeenth century.   Height 7¾″

55. Tyg. The red body is decorated with moulded ornaments as well as trailed slip. Made at Wrotham and dated 1695.   Height 7″

56. Posset Pot made of buff coloured clay with feathered slip decoration in dark red. Round the top is the name Thomas Heath and the date 1698. Made in Staffordshire.   Height 4¾″

Plaque made of red clay with a yellow glaze. The effect of this colour combination is a brilliant burnt orange. The design in relief was probably impressed with a paste roller. The design is obviously made as a repeat pattern, for the lizard on the extreme right-hand side would match neatly with the tail of the lizard on the left. Perhaps it was intended to be a continuous frieze. The top is pierced for suspension. The tile or plaque is said to have come from Wattisfield in Suffolk, and it is believed to be eighteenth century.

Height 13"

58   *Fitzwilliam Museum*   59   *Stoke-on-Trent Museum*

Teapot made of buff coloured ware with the decoration in light and dark reds and white. Glazed with yellow lead glaze. Made in Staffordshire in the early eighteenth century.   Height 8½″

Large Circular Dish of buff coloured ware decorated with dark red slip. Made in Staffordshire in the early eighteenth century.   Dia. 16½″

60   *Victoria & Albert Museum*   61   *Victoria & Albert Museum*

Tyg, decorated with trailed slip with bands of feathering. Made in Staffordshire in the late seventeenth or early eighteenth century Height 4⅛″

Tyg of buff coloured ware with brown trailed slip dotted with white and bands of combed slip. Made in Staffordshire. 1701. Height 4¼″

62

62. Circular Dish the body of which is made of an agate ware of red and buff, coated on the upper side with white slip. The design is cut through the slip and the whole is glazed with a straw coloured glaze. Made in Staffordshire about 1760.   Dia. 12¾″

63

63. Cradle, decorated with trailed slip. These cradles were made for gifts at christenings. Made in Staffordshire about 1700.   Length 10″

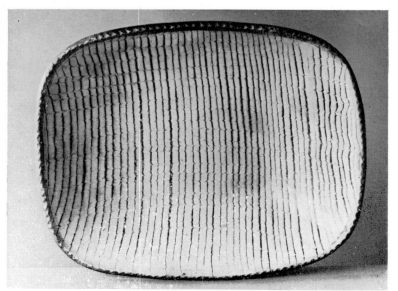

64

64. Baking Dish, ornamented with combed slip. Lines of slip were first trailed across the surface at regular intervals, and then a wire was drawn across the surface of the dish from one side to the other and back again. This drew the slip out in a fine point where the wire had touched it.   Length 20½″

Fitzwilliam Museum

65

Baking Dish made of hard red earthenware, with a trailed decoration in white slip under a yellow glaze. Probably from Tickenhall in Derbyshire, where good slipware was made in the eighteenth century. Length 16¾″

66   John Hadfield Esq   67   Fitzwilliam Museum

Small Flask made of a hard red earthenware, trailed with white slip and glazed to within about an inch of the base with a yellow lead glaze. Possibly from Burton-in-Lonsdale, Yorkshire.   Height 5″

Jar made of a dark red bodied earthenware with the decoration in greenish grey slip, outlined in white and covered with a deep yellow glaze. There are six hounds, a hare and a stag on the side of the jar. Made in Staffordshire about 1700. Height 5⅛″

68. Posset Pot with a lid. The dark red body is decorated with a scratched or incised decoration under a dark brown glaze. The name SARAH BENNET, the initials M M and the date 1724 are written round the lid. Probably made in Wiltshire.

Height 9″

69. Goblet with a lid made of red ware with an incised decoration under a mottled brown (stained with manganese) lead glaze. Round the top is the inscription 'Com good weman drink of the best ione my lady and all the rest 1718'. Made near Salisbury.

Height 11″

70. Jar of dark red ware glazed with an olive green glaze. Marked with the initials W W (probably standing for William Wedgwood). This member of the Wedgwood family settled in Yearsley in the North Riding of Yorkshire, and his pottery made pitchers, pancheons and cisterns easily recognisable by the dark olive coloured glaze.

Height 13″

71   *Royal Albert Memorial Museum, Exeter*

Devon harvest Pitcher. Made of a brown earthenware coated with white slip and sgraffito decorated. Glazed with a yellow lead glaze. The Royal Motto reads 'HONE SOET QUE MAL Y PENSE' and below is the inscription:

> 'Harvis is com all bissey
> Now Mackin your
> Barley mow when men do
> Laber hard and swet good
> Ale is better far than meet
>   Bideford April 28 1775 M+W'

Round the base is 'Deu et mon Drots 1775'

Height 13½″

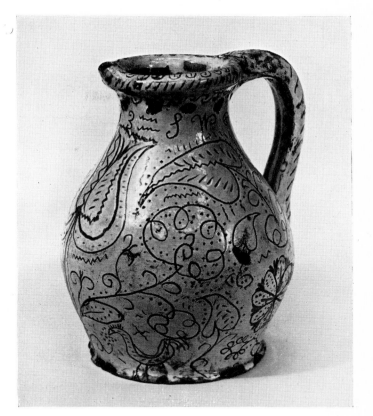

72   *Willett Collection*

Puzzle Jug with sgraffito decoration. The body is dark red covered in white slip and glazed with a yellow glaze. Round the neck is inscribed I B 1793. Made at Ilminster in Somerset.

Height 8¼″

73. Sussex (Chailey) Spirit Flask. Made of a red clay body with incised and impressed decoration, partly made up of printers' flowers inlaid with white clay and glazed with a yellow glaze. On the obverse, within an ornamental border is the verse:

> 'Wine cheers the heart
> and warms the blood
> and at this season's migh
> ty good'

Beneath are the crossed branches and along the edge the words 'SOUTH CHAILEY POTTREY'.   Height 4⅞″

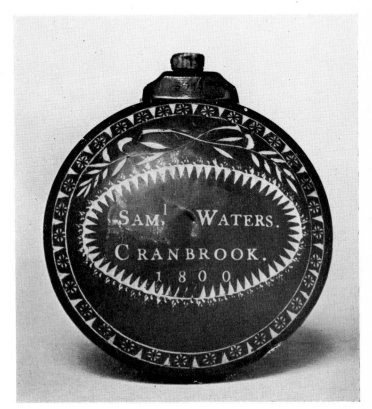

C

74   *British Museum*

Bust of Prince Rupert by John Dwight of Fulham, made about 1670-80.   Height 24″

IV. Stoneware

STONEWARE OF THE 17TH AND 18TH CENTURIES FROM FULHAM, NOTTINGHAM AND STAFFORDSHIRE

Stoneware is made from plastic clay and sand. It is fired to such a high temperature that it is partly vitrified and is impervious to liquids. It was sometimes glazed with common salt, which was thrown into the kiln when it was at full heat. The salt volatilized and reacted on the water vapour from the drying clay to form a silicate of soda, which gave the ware its characteristic glaze. It was first made in the Middle Ages in Germany on the Lower Rhine and quantities of this ware were exported to England in the sixteenth and seventeenth centuries.

Stoneware was first made in this country in 1672, when John Dwight, M.A. Oxon., and at one time secretary to the Bishop of Chester, founded the Fulham Pottery. In the previous year Dwight had obtained a warrant from Charles II for making 'Transparent earthenware or china, and of stoneware vulgarly called Cologne ware'. At Fulham,

Dwight started production with copies of German wine jugs which had a bearded face cast on the front. These were commonly called Greybeards or Bellarmines, after Cardinal Bellarmine, whose controversial writings so upset the Reformed Church in the Netherlands. The stoneware with which Dwight modelled his figures and portrait busts is of a cold putty colour, and is remarkable for its precision of modelling. In addition he made jugs and mugs and vessels in various coloured clays or 'agate' ware. He also made red clay teapots in imitation of the Chinese Yi Hsing ware, that was then being imported into this country in the chests of tea.

In 1693 Dwight put in hand lawsuits against a number of potters for infringing his patent. Amongst them were three potters called Wedgwood, of Burslem, the brothers Elers of Bradwell and James Morley of Nottingham. The results of this litigation are lost though it proves that there was a connection between Dwight and the Elers. Dwight died in 1703, but the Fulham pottery was carried on by his family.

The brothers John Philip and David Elers came over to England in the train of William of Orange in 1688. They were of aristocratic birth, but had learned much of the art of potting, both in Delft and at Cologne. On their arrival in London, they first practised as silversmiths, and then, possibly inspired by the obvious need for teapots, cups and saucers resulting from the ever-growing habit of tea-drinking, they decided to set up a pottery to make 'fine red porcelain'. On Dwight's advice they started their pottery in Staffordshire at Bradwell Wood, which lies some distance from the Burslem—Wolstanton road on one of the few pockets of red clay in the district. In this project they had the assistance of John Chandler, who had been one of Dwight's workmen, and who may have been the instigator of their going to Staffordshire. At Bradwell they found not only the red clay that they required for their delicate work, but also a ready supply of semi-skilled pottery workers near at hand.

The Elers ware is a red stoneware, with a dense semi-vitrified body. The quality of fineness was achieved by the most careful preparation of the clay, its hardness to the high degree of firing to which it was submitted. The pieces were thrown and then turned upon a lathe. Any decoration was applied as a dab of clay, which was then pressed with a metal die made in the form of a leaf or a flower, and any surplus clay was afterwards carefully trimmed off. Spouts and handles were usually modelled by hand. The Elers' ware was always beautifully finished. Their red teapots sold for 10s. to 25s. in London, where David Elers opened up a warehouse in the Poultry.

It seems that the Elers were also responsible for introducing salt-glazing into Staffordshire, for it is reported that 'Eight Burslem potters assembled round the Elers' new ovens, to protest at the volumes of smoke they emitted'.*

The Elers left Staffordshire in 1710, by which time they had introduced fine red stonewares, salt-glazing and a black ware, similar to the later black basalt of Josiah Wedgwood; and such technical improvements as the use of the lathe, metal stamps, alabaster moulds and the refining of clays. They always worked under conditions of great secrecy employing only workmen who appeared dull witted. However, two young Staffordshire potters, John Astbury and Josiah Twyford—so the story goes—worked for two years for the Elers, pretending all the while to be idiots, and absorbing all the Elers' knowledge and skill.

A fine brown stoneware was made at Nottingham throughout the eighteenth century. (The earliest dated piece is 1700, the latest 1799.) This salt-glazed ware was covered with a wash of ferruginous clay, which burnt to an irridescent brown sheen. It was made by the Morleys of Mughouse Lane—the same Morley against whom Dwight took proceedings in 1693. Nottingham ware was finely thrown then turned on the lathe and any decorations such as scrolls, leaves or inscriptions, were scratched on to the unfired clay with a sharp point. The handles were usually made by hand. Typical pieces were loving cups, puzzle jugs and small mugs and punch bowls. They also made curious jugs in the shape of a bear. The rough surface of these was made by sprinkling clay shavings on to the damp surface. Similar ware was made at Chesterfield and Brampton.

* Aitkins: *The History of Manchester*

75   *Fitzwilliam Museum*

Mug with incised decoration and the inscription: Sarah Hole Novb 19tb 1720.   Height 4½"

76   *Nottingham Museum*

Jug (or perhaps a tobacco jar) in the form of a bear. The surface is covered with small shavings of clay. Made in Nottingham in the eighteenth century.   Height 10¼"

77   *British Museum*

Said to be a bust of Mrs. Pepys. Made of white stoneware by John Dwight of Fulham in the late seventeenth century.

Height 6⅞″

78   *Fitzwilliam Museum*

Drab coloured Jug with pierced decoration. The upper part is mottled brown. Made at Fulham in the late seventeenth century.

Height 3⅞″

79   *Guildhall Museum*

'Bellarmine' Jug made during the last quarter of the seventeenth century, probably at the Fulham potteries. It was found in London.   Height 10¾″

80   *Victoria & Albert Museum*

Jug decorated with marbling and stamped ornaments. Made at the Fulham potteries about 1680.   Height 7½″

Fitzwilliam Museum

Nottingham Museum

81. Tankard, the upper part brown fading to a drab base. It is mounted with a silver rim and inscribed with the name James Osburn and the date 1733. Made at Fulham. Height 9″

82. Toby Jug, light yellowish brown in colour. The crown of the hat forms the lid. Made at Fulham during the last quarter of the eighteenth century. Height 12″

83. Brown stoneware figure of a cock with incised decoration. The base is a drab colour. Made at Fulham in the late eighteenth century. Height 9″

Fitzwilliam Museum

84

84. Posset Pot of a light yellowish brown stoneware. The lower part has a pierced outer casing. The upper part bears, on one side the Royal Arms in moulded relief and on the other side divided by the spout, the legend:

Samuel Watkinson   Major
Sarah his Wife   Majoress
    of Nottingham
      1 7 0 0

This is the earliest dated piece of Nottingham Stoneware.

         Height 10½″

A Decantor

A Carved Teapot

A Flower-Pot

A Capuchine

A Mogg

A Carved Jug

Such as have Occation for these Sorts of Pots commonly called Stone-Ware, or for such as are of any other Shape not here Represented may be furnished w.ᵗʰ them by the Maker James Morley at yͤ Pot-House ̴ Nottingham

85

85. A Tradesman's card advertising James Morley's stoneware. Engraved about 1690. This was the James Morley that John Dwight had taken proceedings against in 1693, for infringing his copyright.

Victoria & Albert Museum 87

Fitzwilliam Museum

86. Punch Bowl with incised decoration. Made in Nottingham in 1750.　　　　　　　　　Height 12¾″

87. Wine Jug with incised decoration and the inscription, April 28th 1702.　　　　　　　Height 8½″

88. Teapot with incised decoration and twisted handle. Made in Nottingham about 1750.　　　Height 5½″

89. Flower Pot with incised floral decoration inscribed Nottingham January 25 1703.　　　Height 8½″

90. Teapot decorated with bands of incised lines and crumbled clay particles. Made in Nottingham about 1790.　Height 5 1/16″

Nottingham Museum

Nottingham Museum 90

Nottingham Museum

91. Red unglazed stoneware Teapot, typical of the ware the Elers brothers made in Staffordshire in the late seventeenth and early eighteenth century. The figure in applied relief is perhaps meant for Queen Anne.   Height 4¼″

91

Tea Bureau

92. Pear-shaped Coffee Pot, made in the hard red unglazed stoneware of the Elers type. Made in Staffordshire about 1765.
                              Height 8½″

92

Fitzwilliam Museum

93   *Victoria & Albert Museum*

Horseman, white with dark brown clay details. Made in Staffordshire about
1745.   Height 9¼"

V. Salt Glaze

DRAB, WHITE AND DECORATED SALT GLAZED STONEWARE OF THE 18TH CENTURY

In the early years of the eighteenth century, a number of Staffordshire potters were experimenting with various ways of producing a ware comparable to the fine Chinese porcelain that was then being imported into this country. Taking a lead from the work of John Dwight of Fulham, they turned their attention to the manufacture of a light coloured salt-glazed stoneware.

Dr. Thomas Wedgwood, working in Staffordshire in 1710, was known to have made a buff coloured salt-glazed stoneware decorated with raised designs of white pipe clay. This is sometimes called 'Crouch' ware.

About 1720, a man whose surname was Astbury, but of whose Christian name we are uncertain, perfected a white body by adding calcined flints to a light coloured clay mixture. This resulted in a ware that was both hard and

strong. Astbury had failed to produce the translucency of porcelain but had made a stoneware that could be moulded with great fineness and precision. Soon a number of Staffordshire potters were making white salt-glazed ware and when the kilns were being fired the entire neighbourhood was plunged into a smoky darkness, caused by the action of the salt when thrown into the kilns, with the fires at their fiercest.

Tableware of all kinds was made in salt-glazed stoneware and decorated with intricate raised basket-work, rococo and other patterns, often with pierced borders. The crisp precision of the moulding of these patterns is the most remarkable feature of this ware. Aaron Wood, who had been apprenticed to Dr. Thomas Wedgwood, is known to have been responsible for the cutting of the blocks for some of these intricate patterns, and it is suggested that he was possibly responsible for a number of the pew groups mentioned below.

Colour was first introduced by incising a design into the body of the ware and then dusting with powdered cobalt, or rubbing cobalt stained clay into the scratches. This seems to date from about 1740 and the ware is known today as 'scratch blue'.

About 1750 coloured enamelling was used with great success. The colours were painted on over the glaze and the ware refired. Often the enamel colours have an exceptionally clear and jewel-like quality. Salt-glazed teapots were often made in the most fantastic shapes such as houses, camels and pecten shells; these, and teapots of more orthodox shape were painted in enamel colours, with many different designs including attempts at oriental landscapes with figures, patterns including birds, flowers and feathers, portraits of the King of Prussia, and the Young Pretender hiding in an oak tree.

As well as tableware, primitive figures were made either as toys or ornaments. Sometimes these took the form of a group of figures sitting on a pew or settle. These are white, picked out here and there with dark brown clay for details such as shoes, eyes and buttons. Other figures, both human and animal including very spirited horsemen, were made in white salt-glazed stoneware.

An agate ware was also used with a salt glaze, both for teapots and for figures. This ware was made of white and dark brown clay carefully cut and blended to resemble agate and it was sometimes enriched with splashes of blue. Enamelled salt-glazed figures are extremely rare, and lack the charm of the simple white and brown ones. There are some handsome birds in the British Museum, but the colouring appears garish.

By about 1770, the manufacture of white salt-glazed stoneware had almost ceased, cream coloured earthenware having become firmly established by then.

Tea Bureau

Drab coloured Teapot with applied decorations in white pipe clay. The type of **ware** said to have been made by Dr. Thomas Wedgwood who died in 1737.   Height 4½″

95   *Fitzwilliam Museum*

96   *Fitzwilliam Museum*

95. Moulded figures of a shepherd and shepherdess. Made in Staffordshire about 1750.
Height 7¼″

96. Moulded figure in white and brown agate ware with splashes of blue. Made in Staffordshire about 1745.
Height 4½″

97. Teapot in the form of a house, with a dolphin spout and a scaley handle. Made in Staffordshire about 1740.
Height 4¼″

97   *Tea Bureau*

Pew group. Modelled by hand (possibly by Aaron Wood). The details are picked out in dark brown clay. Made in Staffordshire about 1745. Height 6″

99   *Willett Collection* 100   *British Museum*

Made in celebration of the taking of Portobello by Admiral Vernon in 1739. Staffordshire.   Width 5¼″

Salt Cellar, made in Staffordshire and dated 1744.   Height 3″

101

102

101. Plate with moulded and pierced design. Probably made in Staffordshire about 1750.
Dia. 8″

102. Jelly mould, made in Staffordshire about 1740. Height 1¼″

103. Moulded Teapot in the shape of a crouching camel, made in Staffordshire about 1745. Height 6¼″

104   *Victoria & Albert Museum*

Puzzle Jug with incised decoration coloured with cobalt. This technique of decoration is known as 'scratched blue'. Dated 1764.

Height 10″

105   *Victoria & Albert Museum*

Jug with incised and impressed relief decoration, painted in blue. The initials are those of George III. Made about 1770 in Staffordshire.

Height 13″

106   *Victoria & Albert Museum*

'Scratched blue' Mug. Inscribed I H 1752. Made in Staffordshire.

Height 5″

107   *Victoria & Albert Museum*

Plate with embossed border and hand-painted flowers in the centre. Made in Staffordshire about 1760.   Dia. 9″

British Museum   *Tea Bureau*

108. Pair of modelled birds decorated in brilliant enamel colours. Made in Staffordshire about 1760.
Height 9¼″

109. Moulded Teapot in a design of pecten shells and oak leaves and acorns. Brilliantly painted in enamel colours. The Chinese-inspired flowers seem curious with the oak branches. The figure at the top of the central shell is meant to represent Bonnie Prince Charlie. Made about 1745. Height 5½″

110. Teapot decorated with brilliant coloured enamels, green, pink, yellow and turquoise blue. It has a crabstock spout and handles. Made in Staffordshire about 1760. Height 3″

111. Teapot decorated with enamel colours. Bird subjects, like this pigeon, are unusual on salt glazed stoneware. Made in Staffordshire about 1760.
Height 4½″

John Lewis Esq

    Tea Bureau

Victoria and Albert Museeum

Couple mounted cn a horse made of cream coloured earthenware mottled
brown, green and grey under the glaze. 'Whieldon' ware. Made in
Staffordshire about 1740.   Height 7½″

VI. Astbury and Whieldon Ware

LEAD GLAZED RED EARTHENWARE, AGATE, MARBLED AND TORTOISESHELL WARES

The lead glazed red earthenware that succeeded the unglazed Elers ware, was made by Astbury, who had learned the secrets of the Elers, when employed by them as a workman. This ware had a fine transparent yellowish lead glaze and was decorated with reliefs stamped in white pipeclay. Astbury, as far as we can see, was the most important potter of his time and was responsible for two major technical advances in the Staffordshire pottery industry. He was the first potter to import white pipeclay from Devonshire and it was he who introduced in 1720 ground calcined flints into an earthenware body, thereby considerably whitening it.

Astbury's thrown wares include tea and coffee pots, mugs and bowls in various shades of brown and decorated with relief ornaments of white pipeclay. The method of applying these vine leaves, Tudor roses, coats of arms and other decorations that he used was called 'sprigging'. The ornaments were moulded in a separate mould and then carefully applied to the surface. Sprigging continued to be practised after plaster moulds had come into use and was employed with great success later by Wedgwood, for his Jasper ware.

Astbury is also believed to be the potter responsible for the delightful little figures in coloured clays of bandsmen, topers, grenadiers and mounted horsemen that are to be seen only in museums and in a few private collections today. Their scarcity value is indicated by the fact that at a recent sale at Sotheby's, a damaged Astbury equestrian figure fetched about £600.

Agate and marbled wares were made by the blending together of different coloured 'bats' of clay. In agate ware the whole body is of blended clays, whereas marbled ware is only a surface covering. Additional colours were made by staining natural clays with blue or dark brown. These variegated wares were made by other potters as well as Astbury and Whieldon.

Thomas Whieldon, sometime before 1740 had been making agate ware knife handles; then he turned his attention to the production of tableware. Much of this ware was covered with coloured glazes, blended together to give the appearance of tortoiseshell and an effect of incomparable richness. The colours were obtained from the oxides which could withstand the high temperature necessary for the firing. Green from copper oxide, dark brown and purple from manganese, blue and grey from cobalt, orange-red from iron and yellow from ochre.

Whieldon must have been a man of some perspicacity for a number of young men that he chose as apprentices afterwards distinguished themselves. Amongst these was Josiah Spode; it is recorded of him that 'He is to receive 2s. 3d. a week or 2s. 6d. if he deserves it!'

In 1754, Whieldon took as a partner young Josiah Wedgwood. While with Whieldon, Wedgwood invented a fine green glaze which was used to decorate wares in all kinds of fanciful shapes such as cauliflowers, melons and pineapples. Wedgwood also continued with Whieldon to make agate, marbled and tortoiseshell glazed pieces. The partners continued to refine the body that they used for their tortoiseshell ware, until Wedgwood felt that it was good enough to stand on its own merits, without the need for coloured glazes. In 1759 the partnership came to an end. Wedgwood started up on his own and began to make cream coloured earthenware, which he introduced in 1761.

Whieldon continued to make his variegated wares, amassed a large fortune and lived to a great age.

113

A group of small figures of musicians, made in coloured clays and coloured with various browns, greens and greys under the glaze. Astbury-Whieldon type of figures.

Average Height 6″

114   *Tea Bureau*

Astbury Teapot, brownish black with crabstock spout and handle. The applied decoration of vine leaves and tendrils is of white clay with an almost colourless glaze.   Height 4⅛″

115   *Tea Bureau*

Astbury Teapot with a fine brown glaze, decorated with applied reliefs in white pipeclay. (The lid is of a later date.)   Height 6″

116   *Fitzwilliam Museum*

117   *Fitzwilliam Museum*

116. Agate ware Teapot. Made of a mixture of white and light red clays and covered with a lead glaze. Made in Staffordshire about 1745.
Height 5¼″

117. Agate ware Cat in dark red, buff and white clays with a yellowish lead glaze. Made in Staffordshire about 1750.   Height 9″

118   *Tea Bureau*

Whieldon tortoiseshell ware Teapot of a manganese purple brown colour. Made in Staffordshire about 1750.   Height 4½″

119   *Tea Bureau*

Teapot in the form of a cauliflower, covered in cream coloured and green glazes. Probably made by Josiah Wedgwood, who developed a particularly good green glaze for use on this kind of ware. Date, about 1765.   Height 4½″

120   *Stoke-on-Trent Museum*

Two figures of hussars. One is salt glazed and the other is glazed with a typical 'Whieldon' tortoiseshell glaze. Possibly made by the same pottery in Staffordshire about 1745. Shown here together for comparison.   Height 8″ & 7½″

121   *Willett Collection*

Whieldon Plate made in Staffordshire about 1760. Brown and green colouring inscribed 'Success to the King of Prussia and his forces'. Dia. 9½″

122   *A. F. Allbrook Esq*

Whieldon wall Vase with very pale greyish green colouring. *c.* 1760.   **Height 6½″**

123   *Wedgwood*

Vase and Cover, marbled throughout in the form of agate. The base is black basalt and the finial is gilded. Marked 'Wedgwood and Bentley'. Made at Etruria in 1776. Height 8½"

124   *Wedgwood*

'Porphyry' Vase and Cover, with applied scroll handles and husk festoons. There are traces of gilding. Marked 'Wedgwood and Bentley'. Made in 1772. Height 14"

125. Handleless teacup and saucer and mugs. The large mug and the cup and saucer are decorated with applied bands of very fine agate ware. Made in Leeds about 1790-1820.

Dia. of saucer 5"

125   *Victoria & Albert Museum*

126   *The late Captain R. K. Price Collection*

Group known as Ralph Wood and his son. Possibly
modelled by John Voyez about 1770.   Height 8¼″

VII. The Woods

WHITE AND COLOURED GLAZED FIGURES OF THE EIGHTEENTH CENTURY

Between 1745 and 1790 a small pottery was working in Burslem, owned first by Ralph Wood, the son of a miller of Chedleston, near Leek and later by his son of the same name. This father and son were responsible for a unique contribution to English pottery in the coloured glaze figures that they produced, for they allied to sometimes spirited and often excellent modelling, glazes of extreme subtlety of colouring. In this work Ralph Wood the Elder was assisted by his cousin Aaron Wood, who was the most famous modeller and block cutter of his day. Their early productions were rustic figures of such subjects as haymakers, old age, etc., and Toby jugs. It seems likely that Aaron Wood was the originator of the Toby jugs, but on what he based them, it is hard to say. Possibly the character of Uncle Toby in Tristram Shandy, which was published

in 1760, was his inspiration. Another possible source was a popular song that came out in 1761 and was called 'The Brown Jug' and was dedicated to a certain Toby Philpot. Or the Woods may have been satirizing the sporting parsons of the day, who were often more interested in the fleshpots than in saving souls. They certainly ridiculed the clergy in two well-known groups entitled 'The Vicar and Moses' and 'The Parson and Clerk'.

The Ralph Wood pottery figures were modelled in a fine white clay and decorated with transparent glazes which were often coloured by mixing the lead glaze with metallic oxides. These glazes were painted on by brush, each colour being separate (unlike the Whieldon technique where one colour blended into the next). The Woods were the first English potters to impress their names on their wares. The

127

Fitzwilliam Museum

128

Fitzwilliam Museum

127. Shepherd, probably modelled by John Voyez and made by Ralph Wood and his son before 1785. Height 8¾″

128. Shepherdess, a pair to the figure on the left. Height 8¾″

elder signed his work R. WOOD and the younger Ra. WOOD BURSLEM. The form of Ralph Wood senior's mark can be seen on the figure of Charity in Plate 129. This finely modelled group is without any colour in the glaze. The Woods produced their figures both with coloured and colourless glazes as if sometimes they considered that the quality of the modelling should be allowed to speak for itself. This figure of Charity has a more sophisticated style than the rustic examples that we have mentioned and it is probable that it was modelled by John Voyez.

Voyez was a Frenchman, who is believed to have come from near Amiens and had already a considerable reputation as a modeller in London where he had worked for the architect John Adam as a carver, when Josiah Wedgwood invited him to come to work in Staffordshire. Voyez worked for Wedgwood in 1768 and 1769 but was then dismissed for alleged misconduct. In the Stafford Lent Assizes of

1769 he was sentenced to three months' imprisonment. On his release from prison though Wedgwood offered to pay him his salary on condition that he would stay away from the potteries, Voyez immediately went over to Wedgwood's business rivals, first working for Henry Palmer at Hanley. There is no documentary evidence as to when, if ever, Voyez worked for the Woods and there is no single piece of pottery that bears both Voyez's and the Woods' signatures. However, there is a well-known piece called the Fair Hebe jug which is signed by Voyez and has all the characteristics of the Woods' glazes.

The Ralph Wood figures cover a variety of types including classical figures, such as Diana, Apollo, Neptune and bucolic groups such as shepherds and shepherdesses, historical figures such as Beckford, and also a number of animals including stags, sheep, lions and elephants.

129. Charity. Made by the elder Ralph Wood about 1760. The Woods made several versions of this group, with varying numbers of children. This figure has been left un-coloured and is simply glazed with a colourless glaze. The back view, which shows clearly the mark of the elder Ralph Wood, is particularly graceful. Height 8¾″

130. The back view of the figure to the left.

129

130

132

131. Stag in a light greyish brown on a green base. Probably made before 1785. Height 8½″

132. Doe, covered with a light greyish brown glaze on a green base probably made before 1785. Height 4½″

131

133. Apollo, with green drapery and a yellow lyre. This figure has the rebus mark on the base (on the left-hand side). This group of trees was the 'Wood' mark. Made sometime between 1750-85.   Height 8⅛″

134. The Lost Piece of Silver. The colourings on this figure are light brown, yellow and green. Made by the younger Ralph Wood sometime before 1785.   Height 8¾″

135. Teapot in the form of an elephant attributed to the Woods. The creature is covered with a manganese brown mottled glaze.

                   Height 6½″

Group of Shepherd and Shepherdess. The coloured glazes used are brown, green, blue, a pale straw colour and black. Made between the years 1760-85.

Height 9½″

137   *Wedgwood*

Vase and Cover, thrown and engine turned. Made of cream coloured
earthenware in 1780. Marked WEDGWOOD.   Height 14″

VIII. Queen's Ware

CREAM COLOURED EARTHENWARE AND PEARL WARE OF THE LATE 18TH CENTURY

TRANSFER PRINTED AND LUSTRED WARE OF THE EARLY 19TH CENTURY

By about 1760, the dark mottled glazed ware that Whieldon and Wedgwood (and many imitators) had been making, was going out of fashion. Wedgwood, the great innovator, turned his attention to the perfecting of a cream coloured earthenware that was to rival in popularity and then completely supersede both the tortoiseshell ware and the white salt-glazed stoneware.

This creamware had much the same body as the stoneware, but it was glazed with a lead glaze and fired at a lower temperature. In 1765 Josiah Wedgwood made a dinner-service in this ware for Queen Charlotte, who was so delighted with it that he was appointed Potter to the Queen and authorized to call the ware Queen's ware, a name that was soon to become a household word, and is still used by Wedgwoods today.

An excellent cream coloured earthenware was made in Leeds, possibly from as early as 1765. Elaborate pierced pieces were made here and the finest of this cream ware is very light and silky to the touch. Cream coloured earthenware was also made in other places including Swansea, Sunderland and Liverpool.

A further development of the Queen's ware was made by Wedgwood, and called pearl ware. This was introduced about 1779. The warm cream coloured ware was covered with a blue tinged glaze, the resulting ware being of a pale bluish grey. By 1794 this was also being made at Leeds and by the turn of the century a much whiter ware was being made in many potteries.

Though some of the Queen's ware was left plain, much was decorated with hand-painted borders of small neat formal patterns based on floral or geometric forms, such as strawberries, vines, wheat ears and the Greek honeysuckle. The colourings were simple, yellows, greens and browns, reds and black being predominant. The narrowness of the border showed to great advantage the smooth creamy body of the ware. The largest service ever made by Josiah Wedgwood in Queen's ware was of 952 pieces, for the Empress Catherine II of Russia. This was made in 1774 and each piece was decorated with a different English view and was marked with a frog in a little shield—denoting the name of Catherine's Palace La Grenouillère.

In 1752, in Liverpool, two printers, John Sadler and Guy Green, discovered how to print by transfer on pottery from copper engravings. They first applied this invention to the printing of tiles and the following document is an interesting proof of this:

I John Sadler, of Liverpoole, in the county of Lancaster, printer and Guy Green of Liverpoole aforesaid, printer, severally maketh oath that on Tuesday, the 27th day of July instant, they, these deponents without aid or assistance of any other person or persons, did, within the space of six hours, to wit between the hours of nine in the morning and three in the afternoon of the same day, print upward of twelve hundred earthenware tiles of different patterns, at Liverpoole aforesaid, and which, as these deponents have heard and believe, were more in number, and better, and neater, than one hundred skilful pot painters could have painted in the like space of time in the common and usual way of painting with a pencil; and these deponents say that they have been upwards of seven years in finding out the method of printing tiles, and in making tryals and experiments for that purpose, which they have now, through great pains and expence, brought to perfection.

JOHN SADLER
2 *August* 1756   GUY GREEN

Josiah Wedgwood was quick to take advantage of this discovery and soon arranged for wagonloads of plain Queen's ware to be taken from Burslem to Liverpool to be decorated by Sadler and Green. This practice continued almost to the time of his death, for there are in existence invoices printed by Mr. Guy Green dated as late as 1794 (Josiah Wedgwood died the following year).

At Leeds, a particularly distinctive style of decoration developed in the form of boldly painted flowers in black and red, though other colours were also used there. The Leeds pottery also sent ware to Liverpool to be decorated, though later on they did their own printing. At Swansea, some particularly beautiful painting on cream ware was done by William Young, Thomas Pardoe and Evan Evans.

These paintings were of flowers after the style of Curtis's *Botanical Magazine* hand-coloured engravings; and of birds based on the illustrations in Bewick's *British Birds* which first came out in 1797.

William Adams of Cobridge was the first person to introduce overglaze blue transfer printing into Staffordshire in 1775. In 1781 Josiah Spode, with the help of Thomas Lucas, an engraver, and James Richards, a printer from Caughley, introduced underglaze blue transfer printing into Staffordshire. The body of Spode's earthenware varied in colour from pale cream to a pure white, and had a fine silky glaze. It is very light in weight when compared with modern ware.

From 1781-1833 literally dozens of patterns were engraved by different factories, showing the influence of many different countries. Many were copied from Chinese designs, others from Italian and Indian originals. A large series of designs were taken by the Spode factory from a book of engravings called *Views in the Ottoman Empire chiefly in Caramania, a part of Asia Minor, hitherto unexplored, with some curious selections from the Island of Rhodes and Cyprus, and the celebrated cities of Corinth, Carthage and Tripoli, from the original drawings in possession of Sir R. Ainslie, taken during his embassy to Constantinople by Luigi Mayer.* This was published in 1803, but no mention is made of the name of the engraver. It became common practice for the potters to borrow their designs wholesale from books of this sort, and the whole surface of the ware was covered with the resulting prints.

A distinctive type of transfer printing was done at Sunderland. The designs frequently included a view of the famous Iron Bridge over the Wear that was opened in 1796, but many other subjects, particularly those with a nautical flavour are to be found. In addition to the picture a verse was often included in the design, and bands of pink lustre completed the decoration. Sometimes the lustre was splashed or mottled over much of the surface. The potteries of Sunderland were producing this ware from the last decade of the eighteenth century until about 1890.

Many different objects were manufactured in this ware, but the biggest trade of all must have been in ewers and basins, mugs and jugs. A curious habit was that of placing a modelled frog or toad near the bottom of a mug, perhaps intended to have a sobering effect on hard drinkers. In the nineteenth century many religious plaques were made at Sunderland, lettered with solemn warnings such as 'Prepare to meet thy God' and 'The Eye of God see'st all'.

Fine silver lustred ware was made from about 1805 in Leeds and Staffordshire and Sunderland. Teapots, cream jugs and candlesticks, etc., were made in shapes borrowed from those of the silversmith and were covered with a coating of silver (platinum) lustre. This imitation silverware became less popular after 1840, with the advent of electroplating. Silver lustre was also used with delightful effect with a resist technique, making a white pattern on a silver ground. It was also used on a canary coloured ware.

Copper lustre, derived from gold, was introduced into Staffordshire by John Hancock of Etruria. It was also made in large quantities elsewhere, particularly in Sunderland.

138

Cream ware plaque, pierced for suspension, picturing a sailor and a lady in low relief. Made in Staffordshire about 1780.

Height 11$\frac{3}{8}$"

139   *Victoria & Albert Museum*

Night Lamps and Food Warmers. Late eighteenth, or early nineteenth century. The food warmer with the candle holder on top is 9⅞" high

140. Chestnut Basket. A beautiful example of Leeds pierced creamware. Marked HARTLEY GREENS & Co and LEEDS POTTERY. Made about 1800.   Height 11"

141. Jug and Cover, of a delightfully simple shape, the only ornament being the twisted handle and the built-up knob.   Height 12"

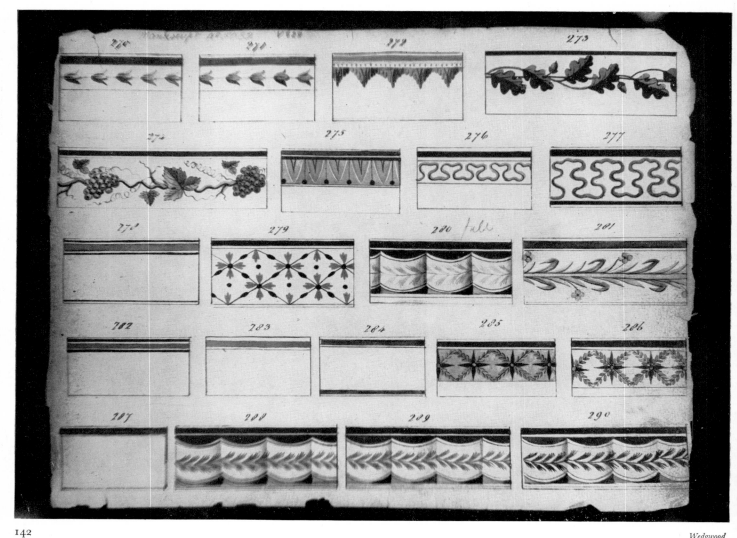

142

A page from an early pattern book of Josiah Wedgwood's. The first pattern book was begun in 1769. It shows the borders used for the decoration of the early Queens ware.

143. Thomas Bentley, Wedgwood's partner from 1769-80, from a medallion modelled by Joachim Smith in 1774.

144. Josiah Wedgwood, from a medallion modelled by William Hackwood in 1777.

Wedgwood'

Plates from the dessert service made by Wedgwood for the Empress Catherine of Russia in 1774. The full set consisted of 952 pieces. It was for the Royal Palace of La Grenouillère and the pieces were marked with a frog in a shield. Plates 9″ dia.

146. An old print showing the showroom of Wedgwood and Byerley in York Street, St. James's Square, about 1809. After Bentley's death in 1780 Josiah Wedgwood carried on alone for ten years and then took his three sons and his sister's son into partnership.

Wedgwood'

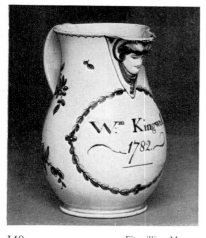

147. Pearl ware jug inscribed General Mercer and Captain Moores 1801 on one side and James Gant on the other. Marked LEEDS POTTERY.   Height 7½"

148. Loving Cup painted in enamel colours, made in Leeds between 1771 and 1781.

149. Cream coloured earthenware, painted in underglaze blue. Inscribed Wm. Kingwell 1782 and made in Leeds.   Height 7⅛"

150. Cream ware Teapot with a hand-painted portrait of George III in sepia. Made in Leeds about 1770.   Height 5"

151. Cream ware Teapot with hand-painted floral decoration and twisted handle. Probably made in Leeds about 1780.   Height 5¾"

152   *John Lewis Esq*

152. Teapot of cream coloured earthenware, decorated in yellow, green and brown. Late eighteenth, early nineteenth century. Made in Bristol.   Height 4¾″

153. Cream ware Jug decorated with flowers and the emblems of the sweep's trade. Made in Staffordshire about 1800.   Height 10¼″

154. Dessert Plate of cream ware painted with a Bladder Hibiscus. Marked Swansea and an impressed spade 1803-6.   Dia. 8⅛″

155. White earthenware plate with armorial bearings, and shell edge. Early nineteenth century.   Dia. 8″

156. Dessert dish, painted in naturalistic colours. Made in Swansea in the early nineteenth century.   Height 8″

153   *Willett Collection*

154   *Victoria & Albert Museum*   155   *Victoria & Albert Museum*   156   *Victoria & Albert Museum*

A double spread from the fourth of the old pattern books of Josiah Spode. The first of these books was begun in 1770.

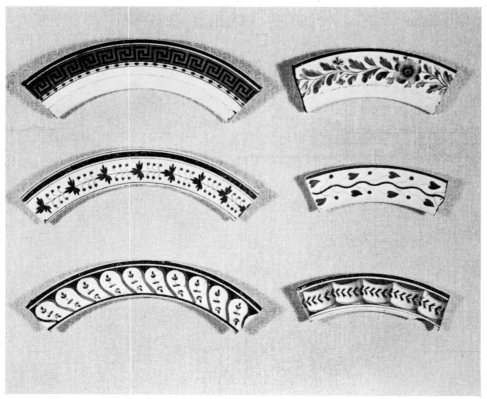

158. Pottery sections specially made for the travellers showing the border decorations of plates in full colour. All these patterns are free-hand painted and traced in various colours.

159   *A. G. Copeland Esq*

Earthenware Plate with a white body. The marks are impressed SPODE—also 2635 in red. The border is of blue Italian pattern printed under glaze in cobalt blue, with an odd centre piece printed in sepia. The printed decorations have been enamelled afterwards in bright colours and gold was also used. Made in Staffordshire, 1818.   Dia. 9¾"

160   *A. G. Copeland Esq*

Earthenware Plate with a white body. The marks are impressed SPODE—Blue under glaze 'Spode' and 3023 in red. A pattern known as 'Tumbledown Dick', no doubt from the precarious attitude of the bird. The engraved outline was printed first and the colours filled in afterwards. Made about 1819.   Dia. 8"

161   *A. G. Copeland Esq*

Cream coloured earthenware Plate. The marks are impressed SPODE. 3730 in red. A hand-painted Chinese-style design the outline being finely traced in sepia and red and the colours filled in afterwards. Made about 1820.   Dia. 9¾"

162   *R. R. J. Copeland, C.B.E., D.L., J.P.*

Miniature of Josiah Spode the first (1733-1797).

163   *R. R. J. Copeland, C.B.E., D.L., J.P.*

Plate printed in cobalt blue under the glaze. The mark is impressed SPODE. This is known as the CARAMANIAN pattern and the design was based on prints from a book of engravings of Caramania. This scene depicts 'Sarcophagi and Sepulchres at the head of the Harbour at Cacamo'. Made about 1809.   Dia. 10″

164   *W. T. Copeland Museum*

Spode Plate printed in blue under the glaze. The design is known as the 'Floral' pattern and is a fine example of the beautiful quality of workmanship of the engraving. Each piece has a different flower in the centre, this one shows a passion flower. It was made about 1825.   Dia. 10″

165   *R. R. J. Copeland, C.B.E., D.L., J.P.*

This pattern is also printed in blue under the glaze and is known as Spode's 'Greek' pattern. The quality of the engraving is again of a very high standard. It was made about 1820.   Dia. 9¾″

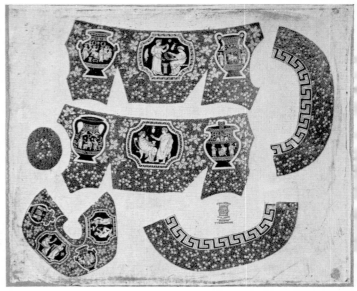

166   *W. T. Copeland Museum*

A transfer print taken from an engraved copper plate showing Spode's famous 'Greek' pattern. The print is for a cottage shaped teapot, showing clearly the odd shaped sections to curve round the sides of the pot, and the sections for the knob and the lid.

167   *Minton*

Print taken from the engraving of the design for the dinner-plate of the Willow Pattern service. This was engraved by Thomas Minton between 1790-93. This world-famous pattern was first introduced by John Turner of Caughley in 1780, in the engraving of which Thomas Minton, as an apprentice engraver, assisted.

168   *Victoria & Albert Museum*

Coffee Pot in cream coloured earthenware, transfer printed in black. Made in Leeds in the late eighteenth century.

Height 10½″

169   *Victoria & Albert Museum*

Queen's ware Jug, transfer printed in black. The design has been taken from an engraving by Hogarth. Made in Staffordshire about 1780.   Height 9½″

170   *Willett Collection*

Canary coloured earthenware Jug, transfer printed in black. Made to commemorate the Battle of the Nile in 1798. Probably made in Staffordshire about 1798.   Height 8″

171   *Fitzwilliam Museum*

Tile, with transfer decoration printed on top of the glaze. Signed J. Sadler, Liverpool and made about 1765. Printed in black.   5″ square

172   *Fitzwilliam Museum*

Tile with black transfer printed decoration, applied over the glaze. Signed J. Sadler and made in Liverpool about 1765.   5″ square

173   *Fitzwilliam Museum*

Another design for a tile, this time printed in red. Made in Liverpool about 1775 by Sadler and Green.   5″ square

174   *Fitzwilliam Museum*

This design is also printed in red and made about the same time, 1775.   5″ square

175   *Hugh Green Esq*

Wedgwood Queen's ware Plate. Transfer printed in black with a design of a collier brig. Made in Staffordshire and probably printed in Liverpool about 1780.   Dia. 9¾"

176   *Victoria & Albert Museum*

Wedgwood Queen's ware Plate. Transfer printed in red with a design known as The Tiger and the Fox. Made about 1775.
     Dia. 10"

177   *Victoria & Albert Museum*

Cream coloured earthenware Jug, transfer printed in black and painted in blue, green and yellow. Made at Liverpool and dated 1804.   Height 7"

Much of this ware was decorated for the North American market. For instance No. 177 has on the reverse side the American eagle and fifteen stars and the motto 'E PLURIBUS UNUM', also the words 'Peace, Commerce and honest Friendship with all

178   *Victoria & Albert Museum*

Cream coloured earthenware Jug, transfer printed in black.
     Height 7½"

Nations—Entangling Alliances with none—JEFFERSON. Anno Domini 1804'. This quotation is from the inaugural address of Thomas Jefferson, President of the United States 1801-9.

179

A pair of early Sunderland Jugs, decorated with black transfer decoration, painted afterwards with enamel colours, and with bands and flowers of pink lustre. One side of the jugs shows the famous Iron Bridge over the River Wear at Sunderland, and the other side shows a version of the Farmer's Arms. Made in Sunderland at the end of the eighteenth century. Height 8½″

181   *John Lewis Esq*

Two small Jugs decorated in pink lustre; one with a free-hand painting of a house in a landscape, in the style typical of the Patterson Pottery, Sheriff Hill, Newcastle. The other with transfer decoration is very similar in shape. Possibly both made at Newcastle in the early nineteenth century

Smallest jug 4¼″ high

180. Cream ware Jug with a blue tinged glaze, decorated with bands of silver lustre and transfer printed medallions, printed in black and coloured with enamel colours, pink, yellow, blue and green. Probably made in Staffordshire about 1810.

Height 5½″

180

John Lewis Esq

182

Sunderland Museum

A Collection of Sunderland Jugs. The top row are all from the Garrison Pottery, the second from the right is marked Dixon and Co, Sunderland 1813. The jug on the bottom row on the left is from Dawson's Pottery, the centre probably Garrison Pottery and the 'Crimea' Jug on the right-hand bottom side is from Scott's Pottery.   The largest of the jugs is $10\frac{3}{4}''$ high

183

Sunderland Museum

Mug decorated in pink lustre and black transfer print coloured with enamel colours. Made in Sunderland about 1810.

Height $5\frac{1}{4}''$

184

John Lewis Esq

Mug of white earthenware decorated with black transfer medallion coloured with enamel colours and inscribed to the memory of Grace Darling the Northumbrian heroine who died in 1842. Made 1842-3 probably in Sunderland.   Height 4''

185. A collection of copper lustred ware showing different treatments of decoration. Made in Sunderland in the early nineteenth century. The largest jug is $6\frac{1}{4}''$ high and the shaving dish is $13\frac{1}{2}''$ long.

186. Copper lustre Cup, with the central white band decorated with a lilac transfer panel on either side, showing Faith and Hope. Probably made in Staffordshire about 1810. Height $4\frac{1}{2}''$

187 *Sunderland Museum*

Group of silver lustred ware, made in imitation of silverware. Made in Sunderland about 1820-30. By about 1840 electroplating had been invented and the production of this kind of silver lustred ware ceased shortly afterwards. Teapot 6⅓″ high

188 *British Museum*

Fine white earthenware statuette of a Hussar, coated with silver lustre. Probably made by Richard Wilson at Hanley about 1800. Height 10¼″

189 *Mrs John Lewis*

Silver lustre Jug, decorated with a resist pattern. Made in Staffordshire about 1810. Height 4¾″

Wedgwood

One of a pair of Vases in blue and white Jasper ware. Marked Wedgwood
and made in 1789.   Height 8"

IX. *Black Basalt and Jasper Ware*

FINE STONEWARES OF THE EIGHTEENTH CENTURY

Josiah Wedgwood was a tireless experimenter. He was always trying to improve the techniques of pottery making. In his early days, when he was apprenticed to Whieldon, they had made experiments together with the Egyptian black stoneware, as they called it. Later on, after having perfected his Queen's ware, he again turned to black stoneware and from about 1764-66 he worked on the improvement of the black basalt ware for which he is well known today. This was made of the native clay and ground ironstone with the addition of ochre and oxide of manganese. This resulted in a hard fine stoneware that could be polished on a lapidary wheel. In this ware he made many busts, medallions and vases as well as tea services, the vases often being decorated in the Etruscan style with red and white encaustic enamel colours. Wedgwood describing his basalt ware said, 'The black is sterling and will last for ever.'

But the ware for which Wedgwood is best known is the dense white vitrified stoneware called Jasper, and in fact 'Wedgwood' has become synonymous with the blue and white Jasper ware. This ware was finally put into production about 1774 after years of patient experiments, and although he had tried to keep it a secret, the ware was imitated by many other potters (often with very indifferent results).

Wedgwood employed many famous artists including Flaxman, Stubbs and Hackwood to design the classical reliefs with which his ware was decorated. Lady Templetown designed some of the smaller medallions used for buckles and brooches. Although blue and white was the most popular colour combination, the other colours also used were a sage green, a soft bamboo yellow, lilac, pink and black.

Since 1769 Wedgwood had been in partnership with Thomas Bentley, a Liverpool merchant. Bentley was an excellent business man and a person of great integrity and it was he who took charge of the London showrooms and supervised the decorations done at the Wedgwood Chelsea studios. Their partnership was only terminated by the untimely death of Bentley in 1780.

Wedgwood

Painting by George Stubbs, R.A. of the Wedgwood family in the grounds of Etruria Hall in 1780.

193 *Wedgwood*

192. Vase with cover in black and white Jasper. The design is 'A Sacrifice to Ceres'. Marked Wedgwood and made in Etruria in 1790. Height 10½"

193. Two pieces from a dessert service in Jasper ware. Blue with yellow and white strapwork. Marked Wedgwood and made in 1790. Dia. 9½"

194   *Wedgwood*

A collection of Jasper medallions and plaques, made in Etruria between the years 1775-90.

196   *Wedgwood*

An early morning tea service in blue and white Jasper. The designs called 'Domestic Employment' were designed by Lady Templetown and modelled by William Hackwood in 1783.   Height of teapot 4″

195   *Victoria & Albert Museum*

Black basalt bust of Shakespeare. It is exactly the same model as the enamel coloured bust of Shakespeare by Enoch Wood that was made about 1790. Enoch Wood is known to have made Jasper plaques, so it can be attributed to him.   Height 9⅝″

197   *Wedgwood*

Pair of black basalt Vases with applied cameo subjects. The reversible covers can be used to hold candles. Marked Wedgwood and Bentley.
Made in 1775.   Height 11″

198. Teacup and saucer made
in black basalt, decorated in
red and white encaustic colours.
1778. Teapot in black basalt
with a lion knob. Marked
Wedgwood and made in 1780.
                    Height 4½″

L. J. Allen Esq

A Mantelpiece made at the Mason factory in the time of C. J. Mason. Probably about 1820-30. (The frame of the looking-glass above is modern Dresden.)

X. Stone China

INCLUDING MASON'S PATENT IRONSTONE CHINA

Stone China was really an earthenware, in spite of its hard appearance and fine body. It was of an excellent quality and was both stronger and whiter than the cream coloured Queen's ware that preceded it.

The first patent for stone china was taken out in 1800 by John and William Turner of Lane End, though other manufacturers scornfully remarked that they had been making it for years. However, when the Turners got into financial difficulties, they sold the patent to Josiah Spode who began to make stone china in 1805. The designs used on this ware were all of oriental origin, some hand painted, others transfer printed in blue, and others transfer printed in outline and the colours filled in by hand.

Other manufacturers copied Spode's work and in 1813

a young man called Charles James Mason patented Mason's Patent Ironstone China. This name had a most convincing ring to it though in reality Mason's ware had no more stone in it than had Spode's or Turner's. Mason's Patent Ironstone China was decorated with complicated pseudo-Japanese or Chinese and Indian designs in rich colourings which fitted in well with the Regency fashion for Oriental taste. Mason's factory produced some large and extraordinary pieces including fourpost bedsteads, garden seats, fireplaces and great vases. Some of these were shown in the Crystal Palace in the Great Exhibition of 1851.

In 1840, Francis Morley, who had then taken over the Mason's works introduced for the first time the use of lithographic printing on pottery.

200. Stone china Plate, marked 'SPODE STONE CHINA' in light sepia. Known as the Peacock Pattern. Brightly enamelled and gilded. Made about 1806.   Dia. 9½″

200   R . R . J. Copeland, C.B.E., D.L., J.P.

201. Two small jugs made of Mason's Patent Ironstone China. Both are decorated with free-hand designs. The jug on the left is dark blue and Indian red with gold outlines to some of the flowers and leaves. It is very light in weight and of a much creamier coloured body than the jug on the right, which is very heavy for its size. Both made during the nineteenth century, the jug on the left probably earlier than the other one.

Height 3¾″

201   Mrs Margaret Rideout

202. Stone china Plate, marked 'SPODE STONE CHINA' in light sepia. Known as the Willis Pattern, it is brightly enamelled in many colours and the narrow border below the shoulder of the plate is traced with gold. It was made about 1807.

Dia. 9½″

202   R . R . J. Copeland, C.B.E., D.L., J.P.

F

Pratt ware jug in blue, ochre, green and brown underglaze colours. *c.* 1790-1810.
Height 7″

XI. Pratt Ware

UNDERGLAZE COLOURED WARE FROM ABOUT 1790 - 1840

This ware is most widely known for the jugs modelled in relief, with sporting and bucolic scenes or portraits of naval and military heroes. In fact the ware to which the generic term 'Pratt' is so loosely applied, consists of white or pale cream coloured jugs, plaques, figures, mugs, teapots, cornucopiae, tea-caddies, dishes, vases, candlesticks, watch holders, all vigorously modelled in relief and decorated with a very limited range of colours. This limitation was imposed by the colours that could be applied under the glaze and would stand the high temperature firing. The most characteristic of the 'Pratt' colours are a rich dark blue and a rather hot ochre yellow. Various dull greens, a pale Naples yellow, a rusty brown and manganese shades and the sparing use of black complete the small palette. The lead glaze used on 'Pratt' ware is slightly tinged with blue.

The term 'Pratt' derives from the fact that a jug which pictures 'Britannia' on one side and 'the Sailor's Farewell' on the other is impressed 'PRATT' on the bottom. In point of

fact, there are other pieces which we have handled, that are stamped 'WEDGWOOD', 'BARKER', 'HAWLEY', 'DIXON, AUSTIN' and 'TITTENSOR', so any of these names might have been attached to this ware. The general attribution of this kind of pottery to Pratt seems to be based on hearsay, and though it is difficult to find evidence to substantiate it is equally difficult to disprove it.

G. Woolliscroft Rhead, writing on Pratt in 1920[*] after he had interviewed a member of the surviving Pratt firm at Fenton and elicited this information, writes: 1. 'There have been six generations of Pratts, potters. A Felix Pratt, presumably the first, married one of the three daughters of Thomas Heath, who was potting at Lane Delph (now Middle Fenton) in 1710. The two other daughters became the wives of the potters Palmer and Neale. The present factory was built on the site of that occupied by Thomas

[*] The Earthenware Collector. G. Woolliscroft Rhead, R.E., A.R.C.A. Herbert Jenkins Limited, 1920.

Heath. 2. The Felix Pratt of the pieces under review considered himself a better potter than Josiah Wedgwood. 3. That this potter was an excellent colour maker: an important piece of information since there can be no doubt that colour is the most valuable quality in these pieces, and the chief quality by which they can be recognized from the many inferior pieces which are constantly coming into the market.'

Of the other potters whose names we have so far managed to find on 'Pratt' ware, Wedgwood obviously needs no further reference here. The only point that might be worth making is that the jug we have seen marked 'WEDGWOOD', which has a picture on it of men in eighteenth-century clothes drinking at a table, is very beautifully potted, with a lighter toned glaze than most of the 'Pratt' ware.

The names Barker and Hawley refer to two Yorkshire potters. Peter Barker was working the Low pottery at Rawmarsh near Rotherham before 1800. In 1804 Barker took over the Mexborough old pottery. William Hawley established the Top pottery at Rawmarsh in 1790. Hawley died in 1810, but his widow, known as 'Dame' Hawley, continued it until 1844, when it passed to her son George, who closed it down and bought the Low pottery back into the family.

There is a very handsome 'Pratt' teapot in the Victoria and Albert Museum, with a swan knob on the lid, which is impressed 'BARKER'. The shape and modelling of this pot is very like the Castleford ware, but the decoration is in typical 'Pratt' colouring (whereas the Castleford teapots are usually only blue and white). The pieces marked HAWLEY that we have seen include the two 'Ralph Wood' pieces illustrated (Fig. 232) and a fairly typical 'Pratt' jug with a portrait of a naval officer on one side and two ladies on the other—possibly Lord Nelson and Lady Nelson and Lady Hamilton.

The 'DIXON, AUSTIN' mark is to be found on a group of figures in 'Pratt' colouring representing the Four Seasons. These classical figures stand on rocky bases, mounted on square white plinths with 'Spring', 'Summer', etc., on the front. These were made at the Sunderland, or 'Garrison' Pottery.

So far the only other piece of marked 'Pratt' ware that we have found is a small figure of a child in a poke bonnet, marked 'TITTENSOR'. This must have been made by Charles Tittensor, one of a fairly numerous potting family, who worked at Shelton from 1815-25, when this figure was probably made. The Tittensor figures are of the Walton type, but in underglaze colourings, usually with transparent glazes on the bases, or of cherubs supporting urns and tablets, of a kind made in Staffordshire and Sunderland by various potters.

A small figure of a goddess with a dolphin modelled rather crudely but in 'Pratt' colours has been found with 'John Pattison 1825' lettered under the base in brown pigment. It is assumed that this Pattison may have been of the family who were potting at Lane End during the early years of the nineteenth century.

In addition to the 'Pratt' ware that can be definitely attributed by the evidence of impressed marks, there is a wealth of pottery figures, some of very primitive modelling and most haphazard colourings, often applied in dabs or dots with no relation to the modelling of the figures. More sophisticated figures such as the soldiers on circular bases (Fig. 211) are ascribed to Pratt, Liverpool and Sunderland. The gigantic sheep with their diminutive shepherd and shepherdess are possibly from Yorkshire as the 'sponging' on the base is thought to have been a peculiarity of some of the Yorkshire potteries. The 'Pratt' Toby jug (Fig. 227) obviously comes from the same source. We have also seen teapoys, figures and relief plaques in 'Pratt' colours, attributed to Portobello and Prestonpans in Scotland.

A pair of fisher girls, with baskets of herrings. These figures are partly decorated in underglaze blue with sponging in yellow and black on the bases, and partly in enamel colours, the pink stripes on the dresses are added over the glaze. These figures are transitional between the underglaze coloured figures and the 'cottage pots' of Victorian times. It is possible that they were made at one of the Scottish potteries, probably about 1800-10.   Height 6"

Hugh Green Esq.

205   *Willett Collection*

Plaque, pierced for suspension and decorated with a portrait of Marie Antoinette. Made in Staffordshire about 1790.   Height 8½″

206   *Fitzwilliam Museum*

Plaque moulded in low relief with a figure of Diana with a hound made in Staffordshire about 1790.   Height 7″

207   *Victoria & Albert Museum*

Model of a cottage in typical Pratt colouring, rather crudely moulded. Early nineteenth century.   Height 4¾″

208   *John Lewis Esq.*

Money-box in the form of a cottage. There is a slit in the roof behind the chimney. Early nineteenth century.

Height 4¾″

209   *Willett Collection*   210   *John Lewis Esq*

Group of horse, thrown rider and dog. All sponged with light olive green and grey and yellow under the glaze. Probably made in Staffordshire about 1790.   Height 8″

Figure of Hope, rather crudely modelled and striped with yellow and brown on a base decorated with green acanthus leaves. Unmarked but almost certainly made in Liverpool at the Herculaneum factory about 1800.   Height 8¼″

211   *Willett Collection*   212   *Willett Collection*

A pair of soldiers, a horse and a foot volunteer. Have been attributed to Newcastle, Portobello (near Edinburgh) and some of the Yorkshire potteries. Made about 1800.

                       Height 9″

An Irishman riding a pig. Probably made in Staffordshire about 1790. The base is decorated with thin threads of clay in imitation of straw.

                           Height 6¾″

213   *John Lewis Esq*

On the other side of this jug there is a figure of Peace. Both figures are against a dark blue background. Early nineteenth century. Made in Staffordshire.   Height 7″

214   *John Lewis Esq*

On the other side there is a more joyful picture of the Sailor's Return. On the front of the jug there is a very pretty free-hand painted bunch of flowers. From the woman's dress the date might be about 1800. Made in Staffordshire.   Height 7″

215   *John Lewis Esq*

On the other side is 'DUKE OF YORK'. Made in Staffordshire about 1790.   Height 6″

216   *John Lewis Esq*

A portrait of Admiral Sir John Jervis with his fleet behind him and a pattern of ramrods and gun barrels round the top of the body of the jug. Made in Staffordshire about 1797.   Height 6″

217   *John Lewis Esq*

An oval shaped Jug decorated with medallions of peacocks,
different each side, and borders of flowers and leaves. Made in
Staffordshire about 1796.   Height 6″

218   *John Lewis Esq*

On the other side of this jug there is another medallion of the
same shape with a similar decoration of children playing. This
is very like the peacock jug and may have been made at the same
factory. We have seen a version of this jug, decorated with
overglaze enamel colours, with the date 1796 painted on the front.
                                                    Height 6″

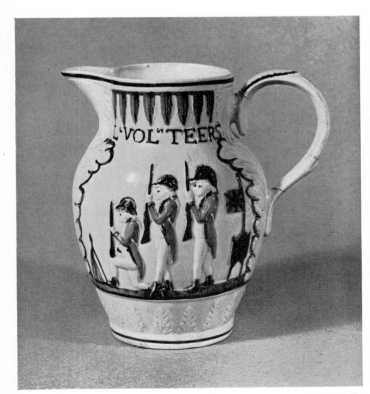

219   *John Lewis Esq*

A Jug dedicated to the Leek Loyal Volunteers. On the other side
of the jug the soldiers are pointing their guns and are about to fire.
Made about 1800 in Staffordshire.   Height 6″

220   *John Lewis Esq*

Large Jug decorated with hunting scenes, different on each side.
The glaze on this jug is a slightly greenish colour. Made in
Staffordshire about 1800.   Height 8½″

221

Hugh Green Esq

A pair of cows with the farmer and his wife standing beside them. The cows are patterned with ochre patches and the bases are sponged in a way said to be characteristic of some of the Yorkshire potteries. The cow standing beside the farmer is a money box. Attributed to Yorkshire and made about 1790.

Height 6″

222

John Lewis Esq

A pair of giant sheep with the shepherd and shepherdess standing and resting their crooks against them. The shepherd is the same figure as the farmer above. They probably originate from the same pottery, made about 1790.

Height 6⅛″

223
Mrs Margaret Rideout & John Lewis Esq

The tea-caddies have upon them caricatures of the preposterous wigs worn at the time. The gothic cottage is decorated with threads of clay and the usual Pratt colouring. Probably made in Staffordshire about 1790.   Height 4¾″

224
John Lewis Esq

Cow milk jug with milkmaid in attendance, sponged with ochre and black and standing on a green base. Probably made in Staffordshire. *c.* 1790. The deer is unmarked and might also come from Staffordshire about the same time.   Cow is 5¼″ high

225   *Victoria & Albert Museum*

Teapot, with a seated woman for the knob on the lid, and a combination of moulded ornament and free-hand painted vine patterns. Probably made in Staffordshire about 1800.   Height 6¼″

226   *John Lewis Esq*

A collection of small moulded figures, decorated somewhat haphazardly with dabs of colour under the glaze. Probably all made in Staffordshire about the end of the eighteenth century. The one on the extreme right may be earlier.

Willett Collection

227. Pratt ware Toby Jug with a blue coat and black, blue and ochre sponging on the base. Possibly from the same pottery as the animals (Figs. 221 & 222). Made about 1790. Height 7⅝″

228. Mug, inside of which there is a large yellow frog. Outside, the decoration illustrates the nursery rhyme about old Mother Slipper-Slopper. Made in Staffordshire about 1800. Height 4¾″

John Lewis Esq

John Lewis Esq

Two Satyr mugs and a Pratt jug decorated on one side by a picture of Britannia and on the other a sailor hurrying home on leave with his ship in the background. An identical jug in the Victoria and Albert museum is marked Pratt. The Satyr mug on the right has a large toad in the bottom of it. All made in Staffordshire about 1790.
Height 5″ (Jug)

230   *Willett Collection*

A boy and girl watching two cocks fighting, in pale under-glaze blues, grey greens, and yellows. Made in Staffordshire about 1790.   Height 8″

231   *Fitzwilliam Museum*

Giant shepherdess with diminutive sheep, a very pretty model in particularly good underglaze blues and yellows. Possibly by Pratt, about 1800.   Height 8″

232. Copies of two famous pieces from the Wood Factory. These are clumsily decorated in rather heavy dark underglaze colouring, and are marked 'HAWLEY' in impressed letters on the bottom. They were made at Rawmarsh near Rotherham, either by William Hawley, any time from 1790-1810, or by his widow, who carried on with the same sort of work until 1844.   The jug is 12″ high

232   *Yorkshire Museum*

Overglaze enamel coloured group, representing a marriage at Gretna Green, attributed to Obadiah Sherratt. *c.* 1830. Height 7″

233   *Mrs Margaret Rideout*

An early group in the Walton manner. Unmarked. Made in
Staffordshire about 1815.   Height 6½″

XII. Walton, Sherratt and others

OVER GLAZE ENAMEL COLOURED FIGURES FROM ABOUT 1790 - 1840

From about 1792, the younger Ralph Wood and his cousin
Enoch Wood, began colouring their figures with over glaze
enamels. Soon many other potters began to adopt this
technique, among them were James Neale, Humphrey
Palmer, Thomas Lakin, John Ellison Poole and Samuel
Bourne who were all working in Staffordshire. Similar
figures were made in Leeds (from about 1794), Sunderland,
Liverpool and other places. It was possible to use a very
much wider range of colours with this method, for the
enamels were put on over the glaze and then the pieces were
refired at quite a low temperature.

During the second decade of the nineteenth century,
earthenware copies of the porcelain figures of Chelsea, Bow
and Dresden were made. These consisted of a figure or
group of figures mounted on a green rocky base or rococo
mound and backed by an elaborate tree with formalized
greenery and large coloured flowers. The name that occurs
most frequently on this type of ornament is that of John
Walton, who signed his name in either impressed or
embossed roman capitals on a raised scroll at the back of
the base. The names of other potters including Ralph Salt
and Charles Tittensor are sometimes found, though most
of these toys or ornaments were left unmarked and their
makers remain anonymous. By comparing styles and
colourings with marked examples it is possible to narrow
down certain types to certain factories. Dozens of potters
were engaged on the production of these toys, which they
made by the hundred and sold very cheaply. Potters had no

compunction in copying each other's styles and models and they kept no proper records. The manufactories responsible for these figures varied from tiny little pot banks employing only a handful of workers to far larger concerns.

Sales of pottery were often advertised in the newspapers and sometimes included the whole stock of a factory including moulds. This may account for the fact that it is possible to come across several figures of identical shape, but with a vastly different surface treatment. Obviously a well-finished beautifully-decorated piece would not have been made at the same time and in the same factory as a crude, poorly-decorated specimen.

Many of Walton's figures are religious subjects, such as the Widow of Zarephath, Elijah and the Raven, and Saints and Apostles; and many of them are little arcadian figures of shepherds and shepherdesses, gardeners and cherubs. Though we know very little about the man himself, Walton's

factory at Burslem seems to have been in full production from 1815-1835.

As well as human figures, animals, houses, cottages and churches were made. These architectural models were often in the form of a pastille burner or a money-box, either with a little opening like a door behind, or else a slit for coins in the roof.

Obadiah Sherratt, who is recorded as being a master potter of Burslem in 1822, made a very distinctive kind of figure. These lacked the sentimentality or 'prettiness' of the Walton type of ornament and were altogether cruder, being almost caricatures of brutal scenes (bull-baiting groups, or the unfortunate Lieutenant Monroe being carried off by a tiger, figs. 251 and 252) or quaint figures like the landlord and landlady in the Willett Collection at Brighton (fig 255). Sherratt's business was carried on by his descendants until some time in the 1850's, so it is possible that the pieces he made were reproduced throughout the life of the factory.

Fitzwilliam Museum

A set of the four seasons, made by Henry Neale at Hanley about 1780-90.   Height 5¾″

235 236

235. Bust of Voltaire, by Enoch Wood. Made about 1790. Height 10″

236. The assassination of Marat. A group by Lakin and Poole. Marked. Made about 1794. Height 13½″

237. An enamel coloured bust of Shakespeare, made by Enoch Wood and a bust of Milton made by the younger Ralph Wood and glazed with a colourless glaze. Both made about 1790. Height 10″

237

238. A group of three classical figures. On the left Hygieia, standing beside a flaming altar. Marked with an impressed 'D'. Made about 1790 possibly by the younger Ralph Wood.   Height 9¼"

In the centre a figure of Charity marked on the back 'WEDGWOOD'. Made about 1800.   Height 8¾"

On the right, Andromache in a pink robe with crimson flowers. Made probably by the younger Ralph Wood about 1790.
                    Height 9¼"

239. Both groups were made by the younger Ralph Wood. Elijah is marked 'Ra. Wood Burslem'. Made about 1790.
                    Height 11¼"

240   *John Lewis Esq*

A group of Arcadian shepherds and gardeners, copied from the porcelain figures of Chelsea and Dresden. These were all made by John Walton and are marked 'WALTON' on a scroll at the back of the base. Date—about 1820.   Height 5⅛"

241   *Mrs Margaret Rideout*

A rather primitive early group by John Walton (marked), made about 1810.   Height 7"

242   *Victoria & Albert Museum*

Crudely modelled figure of a shepherdess. Made by Ralph Salt (marked) about 1820.   Height 5⅛"

243   *John Lewis Esq*

Three different versions of Staffordshire sheep. The two on the left are marked WALTON in a scroll on the back of the base. One has been turned round to show the mark. The one on the right is marked SALT. Probably made about 1820.   Height 7½″

244   *John Lewis Esq*

A group of cherubs, made by different Staffordshire potters in the early years of the nineteenth century. None of them are marked.
           Height of the tallest 7″

245

246

247

245. A mounted General, attributed to Walton but not marked. Made about 1825. Height 10¼″

246. Toby Jug made and signed by John Walton, probably about 1820. Height 9½″

247. Large figure of a horse in Leeds Pearl ware, made between 1800-20. These horses were made for display in the windows of harness markers and cornchandlers, horse doctors and chemists selling veterinary supplies. Height 16″

248   *Mrs Margaret Rideout*

A group of cottages; the one on the left is a pastille burner, so is the one in the centre. The other is just a mantelshelf ornament. Made in Staffordshire about 1830-40.   Height 4¼"

249   *Stoke-on-Trent Museum*

Polito's Circus, a large group made by Obadiah Sherratt in Burslem about 1830-40.   Height 11"

250   *John Lewis Esq*

A mantelshelf ornament with a solemn warning in a fat-face type (*c.* 1808). Probably made in Staffordshire about 1810-20.   Height 9¼"

251

251. Bull-baiting group, made in Staffordshire by Obadiah Sherratt about 1830-40.
Height 11″

252. Lieutenant Monroe being carried off by a tiger. This gruesome happening occurred somewhere near Calcutta on 2nd December, 1792, and this group may have been one of the earliest of Sherratt's large groups. Though the date has been suggested as 1830.
Height 9¾″

253   *Willett Collection*

It is difficult to know quite what interpretation to put on the moral significance of this group. They are all very tidy but they look profoundly depressed. Perhaps made by Sherratt about 1830.

Height 7¾″

254   *Willett Collection*

From the style of the lady's clothes this might be dated about 1810-1820. Rather in the style of Walton, but unmarked. A similar group in the Fitzwilliam Museum has the word PERSWAITION on it.

Height 8″

255   *Willett Collection*

Pair of figures almost certainly made by Sherratt, about 1820. The lady is 7¼″ high.

256   *Wille (Collection*

One of a pair of figures seated in a flowery arbour. The boy is playing a pipe, the girl a guitar. Probably made in Staffordshire about 1820.

Height 7″

257

John Brinkley Esq

Group made in Staffordshire about 1850.   Height 10″

XIII. *Victorian 'Cottage Pots'*

FLAT BACKED, WHITE EARTHENWARE CHIMNEY PIECE ORNAMENTS DECORATED WITH

ENAMEL COLOURS

From about the beginning of Queen Victoria's reign, quite a new and distinctive type of pottery figure was manufactured. This was unlike any kind of ornament that had been made before, both in form and style and in the actual body of the ware itself.

These mantelshelf ornaments must have been made for a large and unsophisticated market, for the parlours of cottages and the kitchens and school-rooms of the well-to-do. They were made of white clay with a shiny colourless glaze. They were very simply though ingeniously modelled, having an almost flat back and usually being mounted on a simple oval base that was much more part of the figure than were the rocky or square bases of the preceding period.

The most distinctive colours used on these figures were a

striking rich dark blue, pink, orange, green and black, though other colours including gold were sometimes used. Some of the figures were decorated only with black, gold, and a pale flesh pink. The figures were often intended to represent famous people and the base was sometimes inscribed with the name of the celebrity.

These figures were made in Sunderland and other localities as well as in Staffordshire. It is known that a number of kilted 'Highlanders' were made in Scotland, for local distribution.

Models of various breeds of dogs, including spaniels, dalmatians, greyhounds and poodles were made in pairs, in a wide variety of sizes and poses. Particularly spirited large spaniels were made in Sunderland—often with copper lustre patches on their bodies, or lustred chains round their necks.

Among the personalities represented were Queen Victoria and Prince Albert, George Washington and various politicians; reformers like John Wesley; admirals, soldiers, poets, prize fighters, singers, lion tamers, highwaymen, murderers, jockeys, and famous eccentrics like Lady Hester Stanhope; in fact these pottery figures portrayed people from every class and profession.

Fictitious characters were also represented and range from Uncle Tom and Little Eva to Romeo and Juliet. Famous historical events were not neglected and several versions of The Death of Nelson were made. Religious subjects—Apostles, Saints and scenes from the Bible were also popular; and anonymous groups of country people: goatherds, gipsies, fishermen, lovers in arbours or with fortune tellers were made in great variety. Also cottages, churches, castles, all had their place on the Victorian mantelshelf.

The production of these toys must have been enormous, for they were also exported in large numbers. By 1840, in Staffordshire alone, over forty potters are listed as toy-makers, although we have no means of knowing what kind of toys they were all making. One factory we do know a little about, was that of Sampson Smith, for it is on record that he was working from 1853 in Staffordshire, and though he died in 1878 the factory went on producing the same figures. Not very long ago many of his original block moulds were found in a disused part of the factory, some bearing names and dates. This sort of evidence is particularly valuable in tracing productions of this kind of which practically no written records exist.

We do know, if only by the personalities that appear in this type of pottery, that production went on for the whole of Victoria's reign. In fact this kind of figure making was not abandoned until after the first great war in 1918. In 1948 the trade was revived and some of these figures are still made today, though the colouring of the modern ones is not so appealing as that of their predecessors.

Hugh Green Esq

Admiral Nelson, c. 1840. A shepherd and shepherdess, c. 1850. A man, possibly meant for an Italian, with bunches of grapes, c. 1850.

259   *Mrs Robert Bevan*

Abdul Medjid, Sultan of Turkey, Queen Victoria and Emperor Napoleon III, commemorating the alliance between the three countries in the Crimean War. Made in 1853-56.   Height 10¾″

260   *Mrs Robert Bevan*

Although Horatio Viscount Nelson died in 1805, this cannot have been made before about 1840.   Height 8½″

261   *John Lewis Esq*

Queen Victoria and the Prince Consort. Probably made soon after their marriage about 1840.   Height 8½″

262   *Willett Collection*

Queen Victoria and her first child. Probably made about 1842. Colourless except for pink, black and gilt.   Height 7¾″

263

264

263. Flower holder. Lovers beneath a tree, from the branches of which the jealous rival glowers down. Made about 1850-60.

Height 12"

264. Flower holder in the form of a group in front of a tree with a hollow stem. Made in Staffordshire 1850-60.

Height 11½"

265. A pair of dancers, probably made about 1850; and an archer with bow and a dog, perhaps meant to be Robin Hood. Made about 1850-60.

Height 10"

265

266   *Willett Collection*

A pair of highwaymen. Made about 1850 in Staffordshire.   Height 12″

267   *Willett Collection*

James Rush, the murderer; Potash Farm—the house he lived in—and Emily Sandford, his housekeeper, who gave evidence at his trial. Rush was hanged in 1849. The figures were probably made about 1848-49.   Height of figures 10¼″

268   *Willett Collection*

Heenan and Sayers, the prize fighters. Probably made after their famous fight at Farnborough in 1860.   Height 9½″

269   *Mrs Robert Bevan*

The Sailor's Return. Made about 1850. Height 12½″

270   *John Brinkley Esq*

The sheep shearer is a large and very well modelled figure. Made about 1850-60.   Height 14″

271   *Willett Collection*

Rear-Admiral Sir John Franklin and his wife. Franklin died while trying to discover the North-West Passage in 1847. These figures were probably made about that date.   Height 11¼″

272   *John Brinkley Esq*

273   *Hugh Green Esq & Mrs John Nash*

274   *Sampson Smith*

275   *John Brinkley Esq*

272. A pair of equestrian figures, perhaps Queen Victoria and the Prince Consort. Made about 1840.
Height 6½″

273. A man with a deer, and Lady Hester Stanhope on a horse. Made about 1840. (Lady Hester died in 1839.) Jenny Lind, the singer, as Maria in "The Daughter of the Regiment". Made about 1847-8.
Height about 7″

274. A pair of sham clocks, made by Sampson Smith in Staffordshire today from old moulds that were originally made about 1850.   Height 16½″

275. A Watch Stand. The central figure has a crystal ball in her hand and is probably intended to represent a fortune teller. *c.* 1850.   Height 11″

276 *Green and Hatfield*

Pair of Spaniels with black patches and gold chains round their necks. These were made in Staffordshire by Sampson Smith and other potters, and also in Sunderland. The greyhound is probably Staffordshire. Made about 1850-60. Spaniels 10¼″ high

277 *Willett Collection*

Admiral Sir Charles Napier (1786-1860).
Probably made about 1850. Height 9½″

278 *Mrs John Nash*

The Flight into Egypt, an uncoloured group except for touches of black, pale pink and gilding. Probably made about 1850. Height 10″

279   *Green and Hatfield*

Pratt pot lid, showing Garibaldi, the Italian patriot. *c.* 1860.   Dia. 4⅛″

XIV. 'Popular' 19th Century Ware

PRATT POT LIDS, 'MOCHA WARE', 'BARGE' TEAPOTS, ETC.

Felix Edwards Pratt (1813-1894), the son of the Felix Pratt of Lane Delph, whose factory had produced some of the distinctive underglaze coloured pottery mentioned in an earlier section, was one of the first potters to make use of the lithographic process for printing on pottery. By 1847, his factory was decorating earthenware pot lids as well as jars for mustard, sauces, etc. A great many of the designs were done by Jesse Austin, who worked with Pratt for many years. These flat white earthenware pots were made for a variety of purposes; the early ones were used for bear's grease or pomatum for the hair, and these were frequently decorated with a design incorporating bears. The later pots were used for shrimps, meat and fish pastes and were decorated with numerous different designs varying from shells and fishing boats to portraits of Queen Victoria. Still later in the century the pots were made to contain lipsalve and were prettily ornamented with flowers. The designs were usually polychrome and were put on under the glaze. These lids were in production from 1847-80.

Another kind of cheap ware that was made during the nineteenth century was known as 'Mocha' ware, from the type of decoration which was supposed to resemble mocha stone. The earliest pieces with this sort of decoration were on a cream ware body, but the later ones were on a cheap white ware. Jugs and tankards (for use in public houses) are more commonly found today than any other article,

though other things were certainly made. Coloured bands form the basis of the design—usually grey or blue or coffee-coloured, and on this background colour, a mixture of tobacco and manganese was introduced. The nicotine had the effect of fanning out the colour into a tree or moss-like tracery. (It is said that the potters used to chew tobacco, add a little manganese and spit it neatly on to the ware.) 'Mocha Ware' was made in Staffordshire, originating at the Adams factories at Tunstall and Cobridge, but it was also made in Newcastle-on-Tyne, in Scotland and possibly at Swansea and Sunderland.

Another 'popular' ware of an amusing kind originated at Church Gresley towards the end of the century. This took the form of enormous teapots made to commemorate the Jubilee of Queen Victoria (1887). These are decorated with embossed relief ornaments in blue, white and pink on a shiny dark brown ground. The chief feature of these pots apart from their size, is the knob on the lid, which is in the form of a tiny teapot. These were particularly popular among the folk who had their homes on the barges or longboats, on the canals. They are sometimes known as 'barge' teapots. Another kind of teapot made for the same market, was also made at Church Gresley up until about 1910. This had a shiny 'Rockingham' glaze and was decorated with gilt and flowers, painted on so thickly that it gave the impression that the decoration was embossed.

280   *Green and Hatfield*

Mustard Pot with underglaze lithographic transfer decoration in yellow and black on a soft blue ground. *c.* 1850.   Height 4″

281   *Mrs David Pearce*

Jug and Tankard in 'Mocha Ware'. Blue and black bands of colour on white ware with dark manganese brown moss or 'Mocha stone' markings. The Excise stamp is moulded.   Height 5½″

282   *John Lewis Esq*

Red earthenware Teapot, with a black 'Rockingham' glaze. Decorated with a gilded beading and enamelled flowers in white and green. Probably made at Church Gresley in Staffordshire, about 1890.   Height 6¼″

283   *Hugh Green Esq*

Pot with raised decorations in pink and blue. The lizards inside are the same colouring. Outside the body of the ware is glazed with a dark brown 'Rockingham' glaze. Made about 1880 at Church Gresley.   Height 5½″

284   *John Brinkley Esq*

'Barge' Teapot, made in the same ware as Fig. 283. Made to commemorate Queen Victoria's Diamond Jubilee in 1887. These pots were used by the people on the canal barges.   Height 13″

Manchester City Art Gallery

Vase with cover, with a blue and green 'Persian' design by
William de Morgan, painted by Fred Passenger *c.* 1888-98
Height 15¾"

XV. Artist Potters

FROM THE MID 19TH CENTURY TO THE GREAT WAR OF 1914-18

One of the first people in Victorian times who attempted to reform public taste was Sir Henry Cole. He won a prize, given by the Society of Arts in 1846, for the design of a tea-set which he entered for a competition under the pseudonym of Felix Summerly. He started up a company called Summerly's Art Manufactures and tried to persuade well-known painters and sculptors to design for industry. This venture does not seem to have been very successful, for it only lasted three years.

Some of the older firms began to employ artists to design for them. Among these were Doulton's of Lambeth, who, under the enlightened leadership of Sir Henry Doulton brought about something of a renaissance of salt-glazed stoneware. The same firm also employed George Tinworth

(from about 1867) to design and make for them many terra-cotta panels, mainly bas reliefs of religious subjects for the decoration of churches. These were executed with the utmost sincerity and were much admired by the general public as well as by the art critic John Ruskin.

Alfred Stevens was one of the artists employed by Mintons for whom he designed a series of earthenware vases. An unlikely artist to work for the pottery industry was Hablot K. Browne (the illustrator of so many of the works of Charles Dickens). Browne designed the transfer decorations for a dinner-service made by Brownfields of Cobridge in 1862.

Robert Wallace Martin and his brothers Edwin and Walter, who all, at some time and in some capacity had worked for Doultons, set up a pottery at Southall in Middlesex, with another brother as head of the firm. From 1873-1915 they produced stoneware in the Doulton manner, but with their own very individual form of decoration. Their jugs and vases were often in the form of grotesque human and bird shapes, sometimes repulsively ugly. Some of their smaller pieces have a quaintness that is always distinctive. Their colourings were greens, blues and browns of low tone and in addition to their modelled pieces, they used incised decorations often in floral forms.

William de Morgan was perhaps the most outstanding of all the artist potters of the late nineteenth century. He had studied at the Academy Schools with William Morris, and, possibly on Morris's influence, took to pottery rather than to painting. He began in quite a small way, making tiles, vases and dishes inspired by Persian pottery and decorated with animals, birds, flowers and fishes in greens and blues. He also made some fine dishes and vases in a ruby red lustre ware on a cream coloured ground, influenced perhaps by the pottery of Moorish origin from Spain. Although de Morgan produced a certain amount of beautiful work, he never had much financial success, though his work became well known during his life-time. In 1888 he went into partnership with Halsey Ricardo the architect, and they founded the Sands End Pottery at Fulham, where many tiles designed by de Morgan were made, but by 1908 his health had broken down and production ceased. De Morgan spent his time designing and did not often carry out his designs personally. Among the painters who worked for him were Fred and Charles Passenger, Joe Juster and Jim Hersey. The initials of one or other of these artists are often to be found on the bases of de Morgan pottery.

In contrast to the dull brown stonewares of the Martins and the Persian blues and greens and lustred ware of de Morgan, other potters were inspired by the brilliant coloured glazes of some of the Chinese and Japanese ware. Bernard Moore, working in Staffordshire about the turn of the century made many vases in many different shapes and glazes inspired by Oriental work, his technical virtuosity being perhaps more remarkable than his artistic taste.

Towards the end of the century, in 1892, the Pilkington Pottery was established at Clifton Junction near Manchester. To begin with they made glazed bricks and tiles, but soon the Pottery began to experiment with decorative ware under the leadership of William and Joseph Burton. During the first two decades of the twentieth century many famous artists designed for them, including Gordon Forsyth, Lewis Day, Walter Crane, and Richard Joyce. Experiments were made with many different kinds of glazes

and shapes. At one time double-thrown pottery was produced, the outer shape pierced to reveal the inner, the whole being glazed with plain mottled or 'onyx' glaze, though this was discontinued soon after the first world war. Ware was also decorated with sgraffito decoration and they even experimented with a kind of Palissy ware encrusted with modelled newts and lizards. But the main feature of the pottery was in the variety and beauty of the glazes that they used.

As a reaction to the orientally inspired work of so many potters others turned to the traditional brown slip decorated earthenware. One of these potters was Reginald Wells, a sculptor by training, who had taken up pottery about 1909, and produced simple if rather clumsy shapes of a purely English character.

Just before the Great War, Roger Fry started the Omega Workshops, where a small amount of quite pleasant, simply-designed ware was produced. But the war had made conditions too difficult and they were shut down in 1919.

As well as the sophisticated artist potters, there is a small group of craftsmen whose work should not be completely ignored. These are the real country potters; tiny potteries in obscure villages run by one man, or with perhaps the help of a member or two of his family, their survival depending on producing ware for purely local use. These men were artists in their own way, and made their pots because they liked to.

The Fremington Pottery in Devon was just this sort of family concern. It was established in the early nineteenth century and passed from father to son producing sgraffito decorated harvest jugs and similar things in a traditional manner.

Another of these country potteries existed in Essex in a ramshackle collection of buildings at Castle Hedingham, where Edward Bingham worked from 1865-1905. He made rather coarse earthenware mugs, jugs and vases with the local clay that he and his family dug themselves. He decorated his ware with embossed designs or with different coloured slip and glazed them with blue, green, grey and brown glazes. The ware has a rugged charm that is quite individual.

The Rye Pottery was established in the fifteenth century and had throughout its history produced wares of an individual and imaginative nature. About the middle of the nineteenth century the pottery was in the hands of the Mitchell family who began to make 'sprigged' ware decorated with hops. William Mitchell developed this technique to a fine standard of craftsmanship and the naturalistic three-dimensional hops and leaves were glazed with a good green glaze, set off very well by the dark brown streaked glaze on the body of the ware.

286

Tea set designed by Felix Summerly (Sir Henry Cole) and made by Mintons in 1846. This was the tea set that won the Society of Arts Prize and gave Cole the idea of starting Summerly's Art Manufactures.   Teapot 6¼" high

287

Terra cotta panel by George Tinworth, called 'The Sons of Cydippe' and made while he was at Doulton's in about 1886. Tinworth's work was highly praised by John Ruskin and Sir Edmund Gosse.   5' 6" wide

288   *Victoria & Albert Museum*

289   *Victoria & Albert Museum*

288. A piece designed and modelled by A. Carrier de Belleuse about 1855, for Mintons. The manufacturers called this 'Majolica Ware', though it was, in fact, earthenware decorated with coloured glazes.   Height 15⅝″

289. Painted earthenware vases and plates designed for Mintons by Alfred Stevens. Inscribed 'February 1864' on the two plates. The tallest vase is inscribed 'Minton 1864'. They are all copies of the prototypes that were made from Stevens' designs and shown at the International Exhibition of 1862. They were never actually mass-produced.
    Height of tallest vase 16½″
    Dia. of plates 11″

290   *Victoria & Albert Museum*

290. A tankard decorated by George Tinworth and made at Doulton's in 1874. Height 10¾″. Two vases made by the Martin brothers at Southall, Middlesex. Figure of an owl with a detachable head made by Wallace Martin in 1899.   Height 10⅛″

291. Four pieces of stoneware by the Martin brothers. The earliest piece is the jug on the left-hand side with the embossed and incised decoration, it was made by Wallace Martin about 1874 at the Fulham Pottery. Height 8⅛″

The vase next to it was made at Southall in 1886.   Height 8½″

The jug with a human face each side of it was made by Wallace Martin in 1900. Height 8¾″

The vase on the right with the 'vegetable' decoration is in pleasing shades of green, probably made by Edwin Martin in 1903.
    Height 10″

291   *Victoria & Albert Museum*

292   *Stoke-on-Trent Museum*

Panel of tiles with a decoration of fish and lotus flowers in blue and green colourings, made by William de Morgan at the Sands End Pottery, Fulham between 1888 and 1898. Tiles 6″ square

293   *William Morris Gallery*

Panel of tiles in turquoise, indigo, green and yellow colouring. Made by de Morgan at the Sands End Pottery between 1888-1898.   Tiles 6″ square

294   *Manchester City Art Gallery*

295   *Manchester City Art Gallery*

294 & 295. Two decorative tiles by William de Morgan. 8″ square

296

Plate decorated in ruby lustre by William de Morgan, probably at Merton Abbey 1882-1888. Dia. 14⅜″

297

Plate decorated in salmon-pink lustre by William de Morgan *c.*1890. Dia. 12″

298. Earthenware dish designed by Lewis F. Day in 1877. Dia. 10¼″

299. Vase decorated by William de Morgan, painted in blues and greens, probably made about 1888. Height 9″

300. Large lustre jar with a reed pen inscription designed and painted by Gordon M. Forsyth about 1910.   Height 12½"

301. Tall slim vase with a band of floral decoration, showing clearly the influence of the *Art Nouveau* movement. This was designed and painted in particularly beautiful shades of blue by Gordon M. Forsyth about 1907.   Height 16½"

302. Large pot with a lid, designed and painted by Gordon M. Forsyth about 1911.   Height 17½"
Gordon M. Forsyth was with Pilkington's from 1906-1920. He signed his work with a monograph signature of four scythes interlocked.

303. Round-bodied bottle decorated with grey-green lustre, after a design by Walter Crane. This was painted by W. S. Mycock about 1900.   Height 11"
W. S. Mycock went to Pilkington's in 1895 and was there for forty-two years.

304. Grey-green lustre bottle with an all over design of conventional flowers by Charles Cundall, R.A. Made about 1909.   Height 9"

305. Large lustre jar in grey and black with tawny-brown colours in the frieze of leopards. Designed and executed by Richard Joyce about 1912.   Height 9"
Joyce was at Pilkington's from about 1906-1931. He was particularly interested in designs based on animal, human and fish forms. He designed some of the best work the pottery produced.

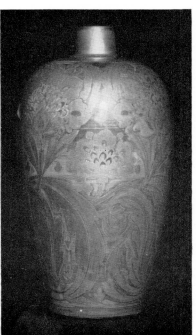

306   *Carter, Stabler and Adams*

307   *John Lewis Esq*

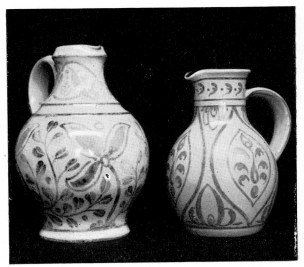

308   *Royal Doulton Potteries*

306. Two vases made by Owen Carter about 1906. One is cast and finished in a red copper glaze with a slight lustre effect. The pot on the right is finished in a greenish lustre. Both vases show the influence of the *Art Nouveau* movement.   Height 12″

307. Vase made by Bernard Moore in fine hard earthenware with a rouge flambé glaze. Made about 1904. Signed Bernard Moore.   Height 9¼″

308. Two jugs made in Doulton salt glazed ware. Designed by Henry Simeon in about 1912.

309. Brown salt glazed stoneware vase, made at Doulton's and designed by F. C. Pope about 1910.

309   *Royal Doulton Potteries*

310   *Victoria & Albert Museum*

311   *Victoria & Albert Museum*

310. A teapot and cup and saucer designed by Roger Fry and made at the Omega Workshops about 1913.
Teapot 6¼″ high

311. Large earthenware jar made by Reginald Wells at the Coldrum Pottery, Chelsea, about 1910. It is glazed with a brownish-olive glaze.   Height 10½″

312   *Royal Albert Memorial Museum, Exeter*

Devon Harvest Pitcher, decorated by some anonymous artist with a sgraffito design of birds and flowers, inscribed: 'Miss Ann Williams Paul may plant and Appolos water But God gives the Increase. Bideford 1866'. White slip on brown body and glazed with a yellow lead glaze.   Height 11″

313   *Royal Albert Memorial Museum, Exeter*

Mantelshelf ornament, probably made by George Fishley at Fremington about 1860. The design in relief shows two naval officers and a negro with cannon and dogs.   Height 7″

314. A collection of Castle Hedingham ware. Made between 1870-1900 by Edward Bingham at Castle Hedingham in Suffolk. The designs are in relief and glazed with either brown, grey-green, blue or yellow. The Essex Jug at the back of the picture shows Boadicea in a chariot on the central medallion, and all round are the arms of Essex families and the symbols of the produce of the county. Jug 13″ high

315. A group of Mitchell ware made at the Rye Pottery by Frederick Mitchell about 1870. The three-dimensional hops and leaves are coloured naturalistically with green glazes and the body of the ware is glazed with a mottled brown tortoiseshell glaze. Jug 9″ high

316. Earthenware dish 'Piccaninny' made in 1938 by T. S. Haile.   Dia. 13"

XVI. Artist Potters

FROM THE GREAT WAR OF 1914-1918 TO THE PRESENT DAY

In the years following the first world war, a number of artist craftsmen turned their attention to the making of pottery. The inspiration for this movement came largely from Mr. Bernard Leach and Mr. William Staite Murray.

Leach had studied the making of stoneware in the Far East, and when he returned to this country in 1920, he set up a pottery near St. Ives with the assistance of a young Japanese potter called Shoji Hamada. For some time Leach made stoneware in the Japanese manner, and then he turned his attention to slip decorated earthenware in the English tradition. Leach trained many pupils at his pottery at St. Ives, where he ran a summer school for a small group of students and teachers of pottery. In the early nineteen thirties he started the Shinner's Bridge pottery at Dartington,

before re-visiting the Far East. He is now back at St. Ives, where with a team of potters including his own sons David and Michael, he is producing a steady output of mainly useful ware of a high standard of quality.

Staite Murray began to make pottery in 1912. Though he attended for a time, the Camberwell School of Art, he can be said to have taught himself, through his own persistent and unending experiments. In the 1920's he also was influenced by the work of Japanese potters. Staite Murray managed to persuade London art dealers to show his work in company with that of the more promising young painters of the time. In this way he managed to establish the fact that potters should be considered as serious artists and not as merely practitioners of a quaint craft. He was not interested in making 'useful' ware.

In 1925, Staite Murray was made the head of the Ceramic Department of the Royal College of Art, where he had a profound influence on many students. In 1940 he left England and went to live in Southern Rhodesia.

The students and others who came in contact with Leach and Staite Murray, in addition to producing much interesting work themselves, have passed on their knowledge and interest to yet another generation of artist potters. Life today is somewhat difficult for these artist craftsmen, materials are expensive, the price of fuel is exorbitant and the purchase tax on their wares is crippling. Almost inevitably they turn to part-time teaching as a means of livelihood. Whether it is a reaction from the machine age in which we live, or whatever the reason may be, the desire to be taught pottery making is very strong today, and the craft is being taught in many schools as well as art schools.

Since the 1930's many potters from other countries have settled down in England and made careers for themselves here. As in the past, we have benefited from this infiltration of foreign talent.

The work of the early post 1914-18 war English potters and their first pupils is very well known, and has been illustrated in many excellent books, and this is the reason why so little of their work has been included in the following pages. We have tried to show as wide a range as possible of the work of the last few years, from the well-known and established potters to the promising younger generation of today, whose work is perhaps unfamiliar. The productions of some of the small semi-commercial potteries, where the work is designed by the principal and carried out by himself and his assistants has been included. The work of a good many teachers of pottery is also shown, besides that of those who are lucky enough to be able to pursue their craft seriously, but as a part-time hobby. We have tried to illustrate the trends of pottery from the 1920's to the present day. These pictures are a cross-section of the work of only some of our artist potters. In a book of this size, it is not possible, unfortunately, to show them all.

317. Grey, rust and white stoneware vase. Made by Bernard Leach in Japan in 1954.   Height 6″

318. Black glazed stoneware jar, with the pattern cut through the glaze to show the brown clay beneath. Made by Bernard Leach in Japan in 1954.   Height 14″

319. A beer jug and mug, made of black and cream stoneware by the team of potters working at the Leach Pottery at St. Ives.   Height of jug 10″

320. A recent group of domestic stoneware, made by the Leach Pottery team.   Height of tallest jug 9″

Though William Staite Murray attended the Camberwell School of Art, he can be said to have taught himself, through his own persistent and unending experiments. He built himself a kiln in his brother's engineering works at Rotherhithe, after the first World War, and began to make stoneware. He was not in the least interested in useful wares, maintaining that the work of a potter was as important as that of a painter, and he produced much highly individualistic work.

322. Stoneware bowl made by Heber Mathews with mottled brown glaze breaking through off-white.   Dia. 3½″

321. Stoneware tiles by W. Staite Murray. Oatmeal ground with rust-red decoration. 6″ sq.

323   *Reid and Lefevre*

Stoneware pot, oatmeal coloured with rust-red decoration, made by W. Staite Murray. Height 24″

324   *Reid and Lefevre*

Stoneware pot of a deep oatmeal colour with rust-red decoration made by W. Staite Murray. Height 30″

325   *Victoria & Albert Museum*

Stoneware pot made by W. Staite Murray about 1938. Height 11½″

326. Stoneware Pot, with rust-red iron decoration made by Heber Mathews. Height 12″

327. Stoneware vase, made by Heber Mathews thrown in two pieces and the upper part pressed to an elliptical form with rolled edge at the top. It has a very pale oatmeal body with a translucent glaze. Height 21″

Heber Mathews studied as a painter and became a student of Staite Murray's in 1927-31. In 1931 he established his own pottery studio. He is now the Principal of the School of Art, Woolwich Polytechnic, and head of the ceramic department. His work is owned by the V. & A. Museum as well as many galleries abroad.

328 *Victoria & Albert Museum*

Stoneware cider jar made by Michael Cardew about 1950.
Height 12½"

329 *Victoria & Albert Museum*

Large earthenware jar with slip decoration made by Michael Cardew.
Height 14⅜"

Michael Cardew learned to throw at the Braunton Pottery in Devon. He then joined the Leach pottery for three years, before buying a pottery of his own, at Winchcombe in Gloucestershire. This pottery had a kiln large enough to hold up to three thousand pieces, which Cardew's remarkable energy and drive enabled him to fill every two or three months. He made mainly useful slip decorated earthenware in the English tradition. In 1939 he moved to Wenford Bridge in Cornwall. When the war started he went as a pottery instructor to teach at Achimota College on the Gold Coast. He returned to Wenford Bridge in 1949 and began to make stoneware, but in 1950 he was offered a post out in Nigeria and returned to Africa.

330 *Victoria & Albert Museum*

Dish with painted bird decoration made by Michael Cardew.
Dia. 11½"

331. Stoneware jar made by T. S. Haile.   Height 15″

332. Slipware bowl in black, white and brown, made by T. S. Haile. Dia. 16″

Thomas Samuel Haile was a pupil of Staite Murray. He was not only a good craftsman but a talented artist with a vivid and original imagination, well illustrated by the spirited decorations on his slip-ware and stoneware pieces. Much of his best work was done in the U.S.A. where he went after he left the Royal College of Art. When he was released from military service, he again began potting in England, first in Suffolk and then at the Shinner's Bridge Pottery at Dartington near Totnes in Devon. He was tragically killed in a motor accident in 1948.

333-34. Earthenware bottles decorated with black slip and sgraffito decoration with a tin glaze. Recent work by Marianne de Trey.   Height 9″ and 12″

Marianne de Trey was originally trained as a textile designer at the Royal College of Art. She learned about pottery from her husband, T. S. Haile, and went to America with him, where they both worked and taught. After the death of her husband she continued to run the Shinner's Bridge Pottery, where she still is, producing more or less standardised tableware with the help of two assistants. She does nearly all the decorating and the throwing of special pieces herself.

335

336

337

335. Stoneware bowl of a warm ochre colour with dark blue-grey brushwork decoration. Made in 1954 by Henry Fauchon Hammond. Dia. 5½″

336. Lead glazed slipware mug with black ground, cream slip trailing and red dots. Made by Henry Fauchon Hammond in 1948. Height 6½″

337. Stoneware bowl of a warm straw colour with black brushwork decoration, made by Henry Fauchon Hammond. Dia. 7½″

Henry Fauchon Hammond studied at the Royal College of Art under Staite Murray. He was also helped and encouraged by Bernard Leach. He has produced slipware and stoneware, simply decorated in the Japanese manner. In addition to running the pottery department at the Farnham School of Art, he has started up a small pottery at Bentley near Farnham with Paul Barron and his wife, where they are producing decorative stoneware.

338

338. Three pots made by Katherine Pleydell Bouverie glazed with different kinds of ash glazes. Made in 1955. The central pot with a cedar ash glaze is about 8″ high.

Katherine Pleydell Bouverie studied at the Central School of Art and later at St. Ives. She is now potting at Kilmington Manor in Wiltshire, where she uses an oil-fired kiln.

339

340

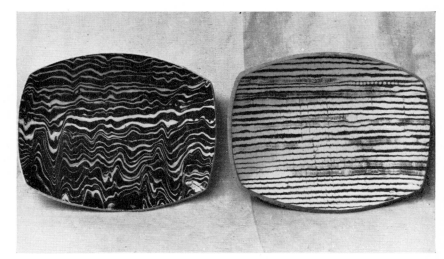

341

339. Stoneware bread crock with an unglazed exterior decorated with tooling and seals. The interior is glazed green. Made in 1951 by Paul Barron. Height 14″

340. Slipware vase and jug by Paul Barron. Made in 1950. Height of jug 7″

341. Two pressed dishes with slip decoration, made by Doreen Penfold in 1953. Length 18″

Paul Barron studied at the Brighton School of Art under Norah Braden (a pupil of Leach's) from 1937-39. He now teaches at the Farnham School of Art with Henry Hammond with whom he also runs the pottery at Bentley.

Doreen Penfold studied at the Royal College of Art under Professor Baker and then gained practical experience by working at the pottery at Wattisfield for a time. She now works with her husband and Henry Hammond at Bentley.

342. Slipware jugs made by Dorothy Kemp, three amber and one black. The third from the left is 11½″ high.

Dorothy Kemp is primarily a historian, but a potter for the love of it. She is mainly self-taught, but has occasionally been down to St. Ives to work with Bernard Leach. She makes slip decorated earthenware in the English tradition and also teaches pottery to the senior girls at the Northgate School, Ipswich.

342

343

343. Slipware decorated with trailed slip. Made by Raymond Finch at the Winchcombe Pottery. The half-gallon bottle is 12½″ high.

344. Stoneware store jar with painted iron in-glaze decoration made by Raymond Finch at the Winchcombe Pottery.

Height 8″

Raymond Finch has spent all his working life at the Winchcombe Pottery in Gloucestershire, first as a pupil and then as a successor to Michael Cardew. He carries on the pottery in the Cardew tradition making slip decorated earthenware and stoneware. Like Cardew, he concentrates mainly on the production of useful ware, which is both well designed and reasonably priced.

344

345. Cider jar and beakers in black and white slipware. Made by John Shelly at the Bath Pottery. Jar 17″ high

John Shelly trained at the Winchcombe Pottery under Raymond Finch. He started the Bath Pottery in 1950 and now employs three other people. He designs all the work and the pieces he actually makes himself are stamped with a monogram JS. Everything else is stamped BATH POTTERY. He makes both slipware and maiolica ware.

346. Oven-proof pottery pans, with brown and black decoration and a buttercup-yellow glaze, made by John Shelly at the Bath Pottery. Large pan 9″ across bowl

347. Large black stoneware bread crock made at the Crowan Pottery.   Height 14″

348. Incised celadon plate and oil and vinegar bottles made at the Crowan Pottery.   Bottles 5½″ high

Harry and May Davis worked at St. Ives during the 1930's. After teaching for a time at Achimota College on the Gold Coast, Harry Davis went to Cornwall, where he and his wife work together, running the Crowan Pottery. They make good hand-thrown stoneware in many practical shapes. Some are simply decorated and some rely on the beauty of a fine celadon glaze.

349

350

349. Cock vase with black and pink decoration, made at the Rye Pottery.   Height 5½″

350. Loving cup with striped decoration, made at the Rye Pottery.   Height 4¾″

351. Flower Box with coloured decoration, made at the Rye Pottery.   Length 11″

The Rye Pottery was taken over in 1946 by two brothers W. V. Cole and J. R. Cole. They produce both useful and decorative ware for home as well as the export market.

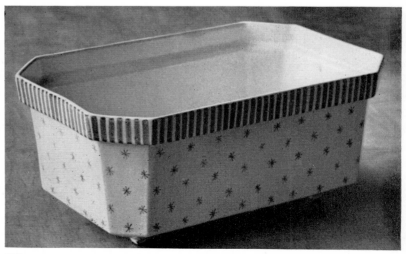

351

352. Coffee pot decorated with ivory slip on a red body, with under-glaze black decoration and a honey-yellow glaze. The dish is black and white on blue with a green glaze. Made by John Solly.　　Height of pot 8″

353. Jar, decorated with black slip on a red body under a yellow glaze. The dish is black and red on a white ground with a yellow glaze. Made by John Solly.　　Dia. 9″

John Solly studied at the Maidstone School of Art, at Burslem and then at the Central School of Arts and Crafts. He worked at the Rye Pottery and with Raymond Finch at Winchcombe before starting his own pottery at Maidstone. He teaches part-time and is also a skilled letter cutter.

355. Stoneware Mead set, with a brown-mottled oatmeal glaze and rust-brown decoration. Made by Geoffrey Whiting.　　Height 8¼″

Geoffrey Whiting spent six-and-a-half years working with a family of Indian potters. Though trained as an architect he gave it up in order to take up pottery seriously. He runs the Avoncroft Pottery at Hampton Lovett near Droitwich, with the help of one full-time assistant. He is a member of the Red Rose Guild.

354. Stoneware teapot with an iridescent red rust glaze, made by Geoffrey Whiting at the Avoncroft Pottery.
　　Height 5″

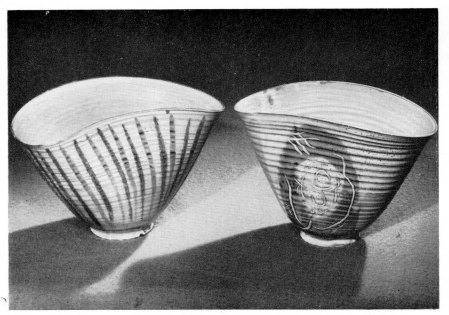

356. Red ware squash vases with a tin glaze. Made by Mary-Gibson Horrocks.
Height 8″

357. White earthenware jug with a copper (matt) glaze. Made by Mary Gibson-Horrocks.
Height 8″

Mary Gibson Horrocks studied with Professor Baker when he was at the Wimbledon School of Art. After working in various potteries she went to St. Ives and worked with the Leaches for two-and-a-half years. She is now potter to St. Mary's Abbey, Buckfast, in Devonshire, where she makes slipware and white tableware for the Abbey's Repository and Guest House.

358. Grey stoneware pot with brush decoration in dark olive breaking to red. Made by Constance Dunn.
Height 6″

359. Stoneware pot with a matt pale olive glaze with darker olive brush decoration breaking to red. Made by Constance Dunn.
Height 7½″

Constance Dunn was a student of Staite Murray. She is married to a chemist, Dr. J. S. Dunn, and together they have made experiments with glazes .She now keeps her pottery going as a spare-time occupation.

360. Stoneware liqueur set with sgraffito decoration made by Irwin Hoyland.
Height 9″

Irwin Hoyland was trained as a teacher, history being his subject; but he became interested in pottery and studies at the Sheffield College of Art and the Central School of Arts and Crafts in London. Now teaching history and part-time pottery at Sheffield College of Art.

361. Stoneware bowl with sgraffito decoration. Made by Irwin Hoyland. Dia. 8¼″

362. Rust and yellow stoneware pot made by Joanna Connell. Height 3″

363
Victoria & Albert Museum
Slipware bowl made by Margaret Leach in 1949. Dia. 5″

Margaret Leach was trained as a teacher at the Liverpool City School to Art, then spent three years at the Leach pottery. She since has been making slipware at the Barn Pottery near Chepstow and then at the Taena Community, Upton St. Leonards.

364. Stoneware pot decorated with black slip under a cream white glaze made by Joanna Connell. Height 3½″

Joanna Connell trained at Sheffield College of Art. She now teaches at the Chelmsford Art School and makes slip decorated earthenware and stoneware with ash glazes.

365. Salt glazed teapot, coffee pot and chocolate pot, made by William Gordon.

Teapot 6½" high

366. A group of salt glazed figures made by William Gordon.

Tallest is 14" high

William Gordon is primarily a sculptor, but has always been interested in pottery. Inspired by the salt glaze stoneware he had seen, as a child, in the Victoria and Albert Museum, he was led to experiment with pottery. He found that the Walton Pottery in Chesterfield were still making brown salt glazed ware, and persuaded them to put up a kiln for experimental purposes. They eventually had to give up the making of white salt glazed stoneware because the losses incurred during firing proved to be so heavy. William Gordon is the consultant designer to a firm in the Midlands.

367. A group of salt glazed lamp stands, in black, white, brown and grey. Made by William Gordon.

Tallest is 21" high

368. Cruets and oil and vinegar bottles with underglaze decoration by Robert Jefferson.   Bottles 4″ high

369

369. Four small dishes with painted decoration on tin glaze by Robert Jefferson.   Dia. 6″

Robert Jefferson trained at the Liverpool College of Art, at Burslem and finally the Royal College under Professor Baker. He now works as a free-lance designer to the industry.

370. Plate and teapot with armorial bearings. Made and painted by Peter O'Malley. The teapot is designed with no flange, to make it easier to clean.

371. Three pressed dishes, with slip decoration. Made by Peter O'Malley.

Peter O'Malley gave up a career as a professional soldier to become a potter. He studied at the Royal College under Professor Baker then worked at various potteries both in England and on the Continent. He is now a tutor at the Royal College of Art. Though he has made many different kinds of ware he prefers making pots to hold flowers, bulbs and indoor plants.

370

371

372. Group of stoneware pots made by Hans Coper.   Largest pot 8″ high

373. Stoneware bottles made by Hans Coper.   Height 10″

Hans Coper, a painter and sculptor by training, came to England
before the last war. In 1947 he joined Lucie Rie and began to
make stoneware.

374. Coffee pot and sugar bowl made of stoneware, brown with
sgraffito decoration outside, white within. Made by Lucie Rie.
Coffee pot 7″ high

Lucie Rie studied pottery in Vienna, and came to England before
the last war. She makes mainly useful ware of a delicately potted
and highly individualistic character.

375. Stoneware Bull and Cow made by Eve Borthwick, who studied painting at Watford School of Art under A. J. B. Sutherland taking up pottery later. Her chief interest is in large terra-cotta groups and figures.　　　　Height 6¼″

376. Dish with resist decoration on maiolica glaze, dark green and black on white, by Ann Wynn Reeves.　　　Length 16″

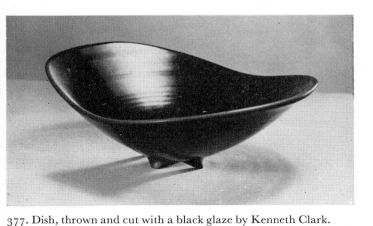

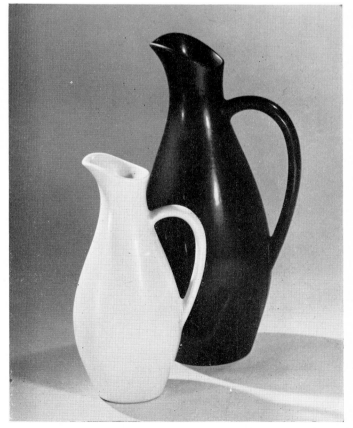

377. Dish, thrown and cut with a black glaze by Kenneth Clark.
　　　　　　　　　　　　　　　　Width 8″

Kenneth Clark comes from New Zealand. He studied at the Central School of Arts and Crafts and worked at various potteries before starting his own workshop, which he runs with his wife

378. Cast jugs in black and white earthenware, by Kenneth Clark.
　　　　　　　　　　　Large one 10″ high

Ann Wynn Reeves, he also does some part-time teaching at the Central School, and at Goldsmiths' College. His work is often decorated with fine turquoise or yellow glazes.

379

379. Earthenware lion with a brilliant orange glaze used with black and white, made by William Newland.
Height 12″

William Newland is a painter turned potter. He studied at London University Institute of Education, Central School of Arts and Crafts and the Chelsea School of Art. He now works with his wife Margaret Hine and they make mainly ceramic sculpture for architects.

380. Vase with black slip sgraffito decoration on a red slip ground.　Height 6″
Plate with carved decoration, white and matt black. Made by L. van der Straeten.　Dia. 9″

Van der Straeten is a musician, painter and industrial designer who has taken to pottery in the last eight years. He runs his pottery at Linton near Cambridge entirely by himself.

381. Painted tile, decorated by Theresa Parnass.
6″ square

Theresa Parnass came to this country from Vienna shortly before the war. She was trained as a potter in Vienna and her work ranges from tin glazed tableware to earthenware figure groups and tiles.

382. Stoneware pots with grey, rust and celadon glazes, decorated in wax resist and brushed oxides, made by Frederick Harrop.

Jar with the lid 6″ high

Frederick Harrop studied at the Royal College of Art. At one time he was the head of the School of Arts and Crafts at Bangkok in Siam. He is now working privately making mainly stoneware.

382

383. Large oval platter made of earthenware with wax resist painted decoration. The colours are turquoise and black with a clear glaze. Made by Margaret Hine.   Length 24″

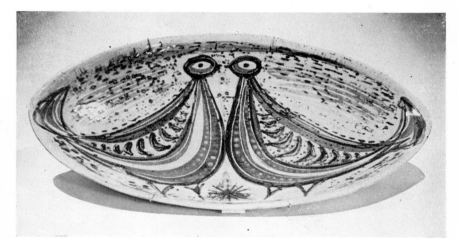

383

384. Bowl made of an unglazed stoneware decorated with oxide colours of yellow, rust red and green. Made by Zlata Kugli. Dia. 11″

Zlata Kugli studied art in Yugoslavia and came to England eight years ago. She now finds pottery a full-time occupation.

385. 'Afternoon tea' earthenware figures in white, black and red clay with a transparent glaze, made by Marion Morris.   Height 11″

Marion Morris was trained in Budapest, where she was born, and also in London. She now works privately making earthenware figures in different coloured clays.

385

386. A panel of tiles made of red clay and glazed with a tin glaze. These are some of the tiles made specially for the Dorchester Hotel by Steven Sykes in 1952. They are either 6″ square or 12″ × 6″. Steven Sykes studied at the Royal College of Art from 1933-36 but learned pottery later from his wife, who studied pottery under Staite Murray. His work is owned by the Victoria and Albert Museum, by the Otago Museum, New Zealand, as well as by various private collectors.

387. Brown clay bowl with relief decoration 'The Expulsion from Eden' in white clay with a clear glaze, by Steven Sykes. Dia. 11″

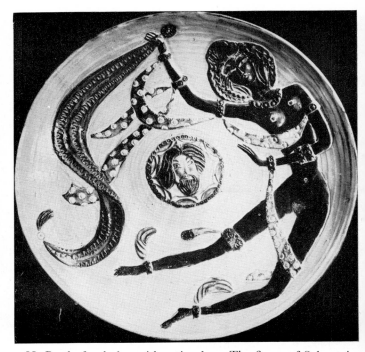

388. Bowl of red clay with a tin glaze. The figure of Salome is decorated with lustre and the drapery is a smoky blue against a whitish background. Designed and made by Steven Sykes. Dia. 11″

389. Two earthenware cats by Nicholas Vergette.　　Height 12″

390. Earthenware groups 'The Goatherds' by Nicholas Vergette.
Height 14″

Nicholas Vergette studied at
the Central School of Arts and
Crafts. He specialises in figure
and animal forms and also
decorative ceramic tiles. He
teaches part-time both at the
Central School of Arts and
Crafts and at the Camberwell
School of Art.

391. Three earthenware pots, blue, black and white; buff and black; pale blue green and black,
by Nicholas Vergette.　　Largest pot 18″ high

K

392. Biscuit ware about to enter an electric oven.   *Wedgwood*

XVII. Factory-made Pottery Today

In the following section are shown a few examples of some of the many aspects of the modern pottery industry. The illustrations vary from mass produced tableware to pestles and mortars for the laboratory, and from fireproof kitchenware to acid resisting containers and stoneware memorial plaques. It is impossible to show in a few pages how wide the scope is today in this enormous and complex industry.

The ware has been chosen mainly from three very different kinds of potteries. The first is from a large firm whose chief production today is of good quality earthenware of a traditional kind, both as to shapes and patterns, though with contemporary needs and tastes in mind. The second is from a smaller firm, whose work, though produced on a com-

mercial scale, is of a high quality both as to ware and design. The third is from one of the largest pottery firms in the world, whose output ranges from salt-glazed pipes and storage vessels for chemicals, to competently designed, inexpensive earthenware produced for a very large market, and individually designed stoneware in their own particular and traditional manner. These three firms have their roots in the past and their wares have developed gradually, as the need for them has arisen. In addition to the three firms mentioned above, some well designed table and kitchenware from various other potteries has been included. This is a field in which the scope has very much widened in recent years.

      Wedgwood

393. The decoration on this plate is a modern version of one of the designs in Josiah Wedgwood's first pattern book (shown in the background). It is known as 'Running Leaf' and was first issued in about 1770.

394. The left-hand plate is made in the Wedgwood Shell Edge shape; this was illustrated in the first pattern book and was issued for the first time about 1770, and has been made ever since. The 'Barley' pattern is also from the same pattern book. The other pattern known as 'Bacchus' has also been produced continuously by the firm since 1770.

395   *Wedgwood*

This cauliflower ware is a direct descendant of the ware Wedgwood and Whieldon produced together about 1756, and Wedgwood continued to make on his own after their partnership came to an end in 1759. It is only recently that this pattern has been reissued.

396   *Wedgwood*

The design for this mug was drawn by Eric Ravilious for Wedgwood's in 1939. It is printed from a hand-engraved copper plate in underglaze black and the coloured bands are applied over the glaze.   Height $4\frac{1}{8}''$

397. This design, known as Persephone, was drawn by Eric Ravilious for Wedgwood's in 1937. It is used on traditional shaped Queen's ware, and is a black transfer pattern with blue enamel.

397   *Wedgwood*

398   *Wedgwood*

Another traditional Wedgwood design, known as Napoleon Ivy. It is reputed to have been supplied to the Emperor during his exile in St. Helena. The pattern first appeared in 1815 as a hand-painted design. This present version was first produced in 1906 in the form of a grey underglaze transfer print, filled in by hand with rich green enamel.

399   *Wedgwood*

This is a new design called 'Country Lane', designed by Peter Wall for Wedgwood in 1955. It is designed to be used on the traditional Wedgwood shapes.

400   *Wedgwood*

This design was originally made by Josiah Wedgwood for a service for the Empress Catherine II of Russia. It is crimson on cream ware. During the restoration of Colonial Williamsburg, in America, many fragments of Queen's ware were found, including this pattern, first made in 1770.

401. This shape, known as Edme, was designed in 1908 by John E. Goodwin at that time the Art Director to Wedgwood's. The moss rose pattern is applied as a transfer.

402   *Wedgwood*

An entirely new range of shapes have been designed and produced by Josiah Wedgwood and Sons. These are known as the Barlaston Shapes and were designed by Norman Wilson, and modelled by Eric Owen. The Tiger lily pattern, shown on these new shapes was designed by Peter Wall. The new shapes and pattern were all produced in 1956.

401   *Wedgwood*

403

403. This pattern, known as 'April Showers' was designed and made by the Royal Doulton Pottery. It was one of the first earthenware designs to be brought out on the new coupe shape, and it first appeared in the spring of 1955.

404

404. This shape was first designed by John Adams, A.R.C.A., in the middle nineteen-thirties. Various modifications have been carried out, including new knobs and handles to the vegetable dishes. The new coupe shape of plate has recently been introduced. The ware is finished in two-colour eggshell glazes.

405

405. This is one of the Royal Doulton pottery's traditional designs, produced sometime during the last century and re-introduced in 1931. It is still in production today. The colouring is yellow, plum-colour, green and grey.

Royal Doulton Potteries

Salt glazed stoneware cat, designed by Agnete Hoy in 1955. Made by the Royal Doulton Pottery Company.
Height 10″

407. A group of traditional Poole Pottery hand painted pieces designed by Truda Carter, A.R.C.A.
Height of largest vase 10″

408. A group of vases made by the Poole Pottery. These were designed by A. B. Read, R.D.I., A.R.C.A., working in conjunction with Lucien Myers and Roy T. Holland. They range in height from 5¾″-17″.

409. A group of decorated vases produced by the same designers as the group in photograph 408.

407 *Poole Pottery*

408 *Poole Pottery*

409 *Poole Pottery*

410

Lovatts Potteries Ltd

410. Heat-resisting stoneware finished with a glaze known as 'Alpine Blue'.

(Photograph C.o.I.D.)

411. Cruet set designed by Dudson Brothers and made of vitrified stoneware in sage green, blue, buff and ivory. Height of salt $3\frac{1}{4}''$

(Photograph C.o.I.D.)

411

Dudson Brothers Ltd

412. 'Cornish' blue and white kitchen ware designed and produced at the Church Gresley Potteries in 1923 and still in production today.
(Photograph C.o.I.D.)

413. Oven and tableware designed and produced by Joseph Bourne & Son Ltd., in 1955. Made of natural stoneware clay with a leadless glaze in black and white.   (Photograph C.o.I.D.)

414   A range of stoneware containers made by the Royal Doulton Pottery Company.

415. Large stoneware vessels coupled together to form a storage battery. Made by the Royal Doulton Pottery Company, for an East African hydrochloric acid plant.

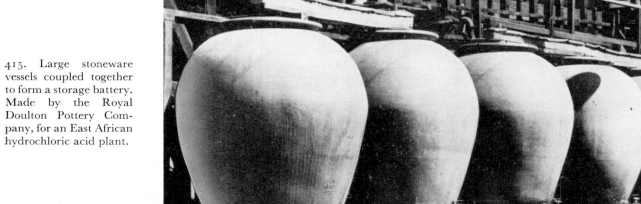

416

416. Pestles and mortars made in a special vitreous and acid resisting stoneware body. These have been produced by Wedgwoods since the days of the first Josiah. They are made in a wide range of sizes the capacities ranging from 2¼ oz. to 195 oz.

417. Coloured glazed stoneware memorial plaque made for the London County Council by the Royal Doulton Pottery Company.   Dia. 2′ 6″

418

Wedgwood

Etruria. The factory which was begun by Josiah Wedgwood in 1760 and was used by the firm until 1940, when Wedgwoods moved to their present factory at Barlaston.

Acknowledgments

The author wishes to acknowledge the help given to her in the production of this book. First of all, to the many Museums and Art Galleries who have given permission for photographs to be reproduced and for exhibits to be photographed. To the Trustees of the British Museum; the Victoria and Albert Museum and the Syndics of the Fitzwilliam Museum, Cambridge; the Librarian, the Bodleian Library, Oxford.

The author's particular thanks are due to Mr. Charles Gibbs-Smith of the Victoria and Albert Museum for his helpful co-operation and to Mr. Hugh Wakefield of the Circulation Department of the Victoria and Albert Museum, for much help and for permission to use information in his *Catalogue of an Exhibition of Victorian and Edwardian Decorative Arts* (1952. V. & A.); to Mr. N. C. Cook and Mr. Ralph Merrifield of the Guildhall Museum, London; to Mr. Geoffrey J. V. Bemrose and Mr. A. R. Mountford of the City of Stoke-on-Trent Museums and Art Gallery; to Miss Margaret Pilkington, of the Whitworth Art Gallery, Manchester; to Mr. S. D. Cleveland, the Director of Art Galleries, Manchester; to Mr. Ernest Musgrave of The Temple Newsam Museum and Art Gallery, Leeds; to Mr. Clifford Musgrave of the Brighton Museum and Art Gallery; to Mr. C. F. Pitman and Mr. Lawes of the Museum and Art Gallery, Nottingham; to Mr. G. F. Wilmot of the Yorkshire Museum, York; to Mr. James Crawley and Mr. Wilson of the Sunderland Museum and Art Gallery; to Mr. Stevenson of the Laing Art Gallery, Newcastle-on-Tyne; and to Mr. S. E. Overal, of the William Morris Art Gallery, Walthamstow.

The author is also greatly indebted to the following people for the loan of photographs and pieces from their collections for photographing: Mrs. Robert Bevan, Mr. John Brinkley, Mr. Gresham Copeland, Mr. R. R. J. Copeland, Mr. Hugh Green, Mr. John Hadfield, Mr. W. E. Hatfield, Mr. John Lewis, Mrs. John Nash, Mr. Maresco Pearce and Mrs. J. B. Rideout; to Sir Herbert Read and Lord Horder for permission to use a photograph from *Staffordshire Pottery Figures* (Duckworth, 1929), and to the following photographers who have all taken photographs specially for this book: Mrs. David Pearce, Mr. Harold Holdway, Mr. Geoffrey Ireland, Mr. John Oliver, Miss Daphné Rice and Mr. John Webb; and to the following firms for the help they have so willingly given as well as the many excellent photographs: to Josiah Wedgwood and Sons, particularly to Mr. Thomas Lyth, Mr. Alan Eden-Green and Miss Kathleen Dibley; to W. T. Copeland and Sons, and particularly to Mr. Gresham Copeland, Mr. H. Holdway and Mr. Smith; to the Royal Doulton Pottery Company Ltd., and particularly to Mr. Desmond Eyles and Mr. Kerry; to Mintons Ltd., and particularly to Mr. J. Steel and Mr. Taylor; to Mr. T. Fox of Sampson Smith Ltd.

Grateful thanks are also due to Professor Baker of the Royal College of Art, Mr. William Low of Heal and Sons, Mr. Lucien Myers and Mr. A. J. Harper of the Poole Pottery, Mr. W. V. Cole of the Rye Pottery, Mr. R. J. Dennis of the Tea Bureau, Mr. Reginald Haggar, Mr. L. J. Allan and Mr. Henry Rothschild.

Acknowledgement is also made of the generosity of the many present-day potters who have so kindly supplied photographs of their work, and particularly to Mr. Henry Hammond, Miss Dorothy Kemp, Mr. Peter O'Malley and Mr. Heber Mathews, who have also helped in other ways.

Finally, I would like to thank Mr. John Hadfield on whose suggestion the book was written, and Mr. John Lewis for constant help and advice at every stage of production.

GRISELDA LEWIS

INDEX

(The figures refer to the numbered illustrations)